Groves Monographs on Marriage and Family

Series Editor: Brian Paul Masciadrelli

Groves Monographs on Marriage and Family

Groves Monographs on Marriage and Family is an edited book series based on the annual meetings of the Groves Conference on Marriage and Family, an interdisciplinary, interprofessional organization of limited invited membership founded in 1934. Groves Monographs publishes work on the leading edges of theory development and empirical research in the field of family studies. Individual volumes are edited by the chairs of the annual Groves Conferences and include peer-reviewed chapters by the conference presenters and invited authors. Topics are timely and provocative with diverse themes.

Groves Monographs on Marriage and Family

Volume 6

Families at the Intersection of Mental Health and Disabilities

Brian Paul Masciadrelli

State University of New York at Fredonia

Anisa Zvonkovic

East Carolina University

Volume Editors

Michigan Publishing
University of Michigan Library
Ann Arbor, Michigan
2020

For information:
Groves Conference on Marriage and Family
P.O. Box 1011, Forest Lake, MN 55025
grovesmanager@yahoo.com
www.grovesconference.org

Groves Monographs on Marriage & Family, Volume 6
Families at the Intersection of Mental Health and Disabilities.
[edited by] Brian Paul Masciadrelli, Anisa Zvonkovic

ISBN: 978-1-60785-708-2

Michigan Publishing
University of Michigan Library
Ann Arbor, Michigan
2020

*Families at the Intersection of
Mental Health and Disabilities*

Contents

Chapter One

Long-Term Care Services for Adults with Disabilities and their Aging Caregivers: A Family Impact Analysis

Karen Doneker Mancini

Towson University

Barbara H. Settles

University of Delaware

Two scholarly and policy traditions have grown up side by side: disabilities and gerontology. There have been revolutionary changes in how both disabilities and frailty due to aging are viewed, served and supported. Families have been a major focus in both fields, but little sharing has been done between the disciplines as to how families experience these changes and deal with them over time. Disability and aging services are often housed separately. In family life, there needs to be many connections between these services and the individuals and the families that use them. The purpose of this study is to examine, using Bogenschneider's (2006) approach to family impact analysis, the implementation of federal and state policies in the area of services for adults with disabilities and their aging caregivers in the State of Delaware. The study presented here included 24 qualitative interviews with stakeholders within the state.

Disability Policy

The first major disabilities policy change came with deinstitutionalization of individuals with disabilities and was fueled by the major roles citizen/family advocates played in changing policy for children and adults with disabilities (Braddock, Hemp, & Rizzolo, 2008). Policies to support home care of children and gain access to appropriate education were hard fought issues. Baby-boomer families fought a system and society that told them that they should institutionalize their loved one with a disability, and many harbor a mistrust of that system, especially after the horrors of some congregate living facilities came to light in the '70s and '80s (Bigby, 2004). Families reported a lack of confidence in the service system that make them reluctant to initiate contact with the system even when resources are needed (Bigby, 2004).

A programming preference among families and advocates developed allowing the affected individual a measure of autonomy and independence from their family of origin in adult life. The preference was acknowledged with the Olmstead Act in 1989 that requires that individual's be served in the least restrictive environment (Taylor, 2004). Paralleling the theory of a family life cycle, approaches featured smaller community-based housing arrangements instead of living with the family of origin or institutions. Work arrangements for individuals with developmental disabilities after secondary school were located in the community and often required simple tasks for below minimum wage. These approaches to housing and work allowed individuals with disabilities to be "launched" from their families in young adulthood or cared for in later life when parents were aged and less able to provide care. The disabilities community has focused effectively on transition planning and independent living skill development for young adults with developmental and/or physical disabilities. Both parents and the young adult saw the process a positive step in keeping with their values (Levine & Wagner, 2007). In addition, transition planning is implemented within the school system and as such, individuals that experience an onset of disability after secondary school may not receive the same level of intervention. Finally, transition planning may vary based on the type of disability. For example, students with learning disabilities received transition planning to work or secondary education while individuals with significant physical or sensory limitations and individuals with developmental disabilities received more focused life skills training.

Another area of policy that is relevant is zoning policy for homes and communities. Historically, housing zoning in the USA narrowly defined families eligible to reside in single-family homes and often excluded non-related persons such as foster children and group homes for persons experiencing mental illness or physical disabilities. In addition, children were excluded from elder care focused communities and subsidies for public housing of non-traditional families (Liebig, Kornig & Pynoos, 2006, Copen, 2006). Zoning and housing development have been changed to encourage group housing in ordinary neighborhoods or new developments (U.S. Department of Housing and Urban Development, 2017). Even so, according to the parents, 7 out of 10 adults with developmental disabilities (AWDs) have remained living with their families (EasterSeals, 2010). Both better medical care and the daily support of families have been accompanied by longer life expectancies for AWDs (Harrington,

Chapman, & Miller, 2005; Mulvany, Barron, & McConkey, 2007). Out of home placements of children and young adults with disabilities have decreased dramatically in the United States and many other countries (Harrington, Chapman, & Miller, 2005; Mulvany, Barron, & McConkey, 2007). Programs to move institutionalized AWDs back into the community have been implemented. Often these initiatives were slowed by the fact that family ties had been severed earlier. People with long-term care needs associated with their disability will likely outlive their parents and potentially share lives with their siblings for more than seven decades (Harrington, et al, 2005; Mulvany, et al, 2007). Many parents of AWDs worry about what will happen to their son or daughter when they are no longer able to provide care (Freedman, Krauss, & Seltzer, 1997; Weeks, Nilsson, Bryanton, & Kozma, 2009; Easter Seals, 2010).

Aging Policy

Concurrently, gerontological research and aging policy focused on the longer life expectancies of both the aged and those who were caring for them. It may well be that by the mid-21st century the elderly will outnumber the young for the first time in history (Bengston, Lowenstein, Putney, & Gans, 2003, p. 19). Mutual support among family members and intergenerational transfers are important family processes. "The fact extended families have retained their intergenerational bonds, even in the face of such significant changes as greater geographical dispersion, higher rates of divorce, increased prevalence of single-person households and single parent families...attests to the strength of such ties." (Harootyan & Bengston, 1994, p. 10) While most of the aging live long lives without having to accommodate themselves to severe disabilities, fragility and new disabling conditions happen as many people live decades beyond retirement (Ploeg, Campbell, Denton, Joshi, & Davies, 2003). So far we have not seen a great increase of elderly with severe health problems and the rates of moderate and severe disabilities among those of 65 have declined (Cherlin, 2010). Over 90% of elders over 65 are still in regular community housing in the United States. About 4–5% of them are institutionalized and the remaining 5% have some assistance built into their housing arrangements (Moody, 2006). Trends for elders over 85 have also seen a shift in that the percentage of individuals in nursing homes has reduced from 27% in 1990 to 13% in 2014 for women and 17% in 1990 to 8% in 2014 for men (Stepler, 2016).

A common reason an elder enters a nursing home or assisted living arrangement is the failed health of the caregiver (Settles, 2007). Aging has several phases in terms of stressors and family coping. Retirement and active life dominate the first part of the aging process (Price &

Humble 2010, Silverstein & Giarrusso, 2010). As early retirement goals
are achieved and health and activity limitations arise, the need for some
care and concern may be recognized by parents and their adult children
or other close family members and friends. Many of these elders may be
dependent on adults who are no longer young themselves.

The themes in gerontology are aging in place, homestead exemp-
tions, and community waivers for in-home services (Hill, 2006). Aging in
place is a perspective in planning that prioritizes the desire of the aging
adult to remain in their own home. These concepts meet the preferences
of many families and appear to be beneficial in terms of costs and benefits
both to families and states. A wide variety of partially and completely
institutionalized private sector housing for aging are available. Just as
in the case of residential placements that include caregiving for adults
with disabilities, zoning and other restrictions have made it difficult for
co-housing across the generations in ordinary neighborhoods (Liebig,
Kornig & Pynoos, 2006). Governmental supports may include retrofitting
and adapting the home for the elder, and in some states in-home visiting
and medical monitoring to supplement familial care. Familial care comes
at a considerable savings to society (Feinberg, Horvath, Hunt, & Plosster,
2003).

Another area of policy is with the Federal Medicaid program
which has strict income and asset eligibility requirements. When nursing home care is needed the Medicaid program is only available to those
with minimal resources or those who accept spending down savings
and assets and/or breaking family ties (Hill, 2006). Medicaid policies
pose complications for couples and families in terms eligibility by reaching into the couples' pooled finances (Caro, 2006). Medicaid regulations
have only recently allowed payment to immediate family members for
personal assistance (Doneker, 2012). The home is usually excluded when
resources are sought or passed on, but the process may be quite complex
(Hill, 2006). Savings used to care for one member of the couple may leave
the couple or surviving spouse without retirement savings or assets.

Key Policies

While there are many policies and procedures in both aging and
disability services that affect families, some are especially relevant for aging families with an adult child with a disability. Table 1 highlights some
policies in both fields which shape current choice in long term care and
living arrangements. Some federal policies cut across both fields. State
level policies are specific to Delaware for the purposes of this study.

State governments implement and adapt policy. The federal gov-

Disabilities	Elder Care
1973 Section 504 of the Rehabilitation Act requires organizations, departments and agencies that receive federal funding to make reasonable modifications to provide equal opportunity to individuals with documented disabilities.	**1965** The Older Americans Act provided the first federal legislation to provide support for elders in their home such as meals-on-wheels, in-home health services, caregiver support. The act also provided funding to reduce hospitalization and support aging-in-place supports.
1983 Home and Community Based Services (HCBS) first become available with the addition of section 1915c to the Social Security Act. Medicaid beneficiaries were allowed to receive services in their own home or community. The programs are written and implemented by the states.	
1990 The American's with Disabilities Act (ADA) guarantees equal opportunity for individuals with disabilities as a civil right. Requirements to provide reasonable accommodations and protection from discrimination are expanded to include all public entities. **1999** Olmsted decision: requires Medicaid to provide long term supports in settings best suited to the individual. **2003** Nine states granted research funding on transition programs from institutions. Person Centered Planning becomes a best practice.	**1990** Older Workers Benefit Protection Act National Institute of Aging formed. National Institute of Mental Health initiated longitudinal studies **1993** Family and Medical Leave Act provided protection to employees who provide care for aging family members **2003** Medicare Modernization Act, now called Medicare Health Support, authorized the development and testing of voluntary chronic care improvement programs to improve the quality of life for people living with multiple chronic illnesses.
2005 HBCS Waivers became a formal Medicaid State plan option. States can apply to have one or more waiver programs. Often the waivers are implemented by different departments within the State. Individuals may only be served by one waiver at a time.	
2005 Money Follows the Person (MFP) Deficit Reduction Act emphasizes community living for quality and cost effectiveness, requires rebalancing funds to promote community transitions. **2008** American's with Disabilities Ammendments Act (ADAA) provided further clarification on the original act. **2009** Evaluation of MFP notes difficulties with implementation, more success when waivers were used to offer priority to MFP participants & greater flexibility (Irwin et al., 2010; Medicaid.gov)	**Areas of State Policy Actions (Hill, 2006):** • Medicaid Spend Down – States provide process. • Medicaid spousal protection - Primary residence exemptions and resource allowance for spouses. • Estate recovery plans - Allows states to recoup Medicaid spending from estate heirs. • Filial responsibility - some states require adult children to provide financial support to their parents. • Miller trusts - Trusts offer an option for families to protect money that would not affect their asset level.
2010 Delaware's Division for Developmental Disability Services (DDDS) decides not to combine the Developmental Disabilities Waiver with the Aging and Physical Disabilities Waiver. (Doneker, 2012) **2010** The Patient Protection and Affordable Care Act of 2010 expands the Money Follows the Person Program (MFP). Essential benefits are guaranteed.	**2010-11** Three Delaware Medicaid HCBS waivers are combined – the Elderly and Disabled Waiver, the Assisted Living Waiver and the Brain Injury Waiver **2010** The Elder Justice Act was included in the Patient Protection and Affordable Care Act to address education and intervention on elder abuse.
2011 New Americans with Disabilities Act rules expanded accessibility requirements for recreational facilities.	**2012 -2016** Older Americans Act was reauthorized and signed in 2016 and included a focus on economic security for elders, coordination of care for chronic illnesses, modernization of senior centers, health promotion and risk assessment.

Table 1. *Highlights of Long Term Care Policies in Disabilities and Aging.*

ernment may be the primary funding stream, but the states have scope in the application to cases and programs (Hill. 2006). This flexibility is increased when waivers are granted. The Home and Community Based Services Waivers are federally funded programs that allow AWDs and elders to waive their right to institutionalization and receive home and community-based services instead. Each waiver dictates the services available and not all services are offered under each waiver. Individuals can only be served by one waiver at a time. The Money Follows the Person Program provides additional funds for the first year when an AWD moves out of a facility.

Understanding both the perspective of services for aging and services for AWDs is necessary more than ever before because this is the first generation of non- institutionalized AWDs to be with their aging parents at home (Doneker, 2012). Service providers may use both sets of policies and services which often require multiple referrals and coordination. There is an interest in cost containment at all levels of government and the use of family or relative care is strategic because its costs do not appear on the books of the programs. In the United States, families provide over $257 billion in unpaid, direct support which approximately equals Medicare spending in 2002 and surpasses spending on Medicaid for the same year. Care comes at a considerable emotional, financial, and physical cost to families and responsibility is not always evenly distributed (Feinberg et al., 2003).

The tool of federal waivers has been seen as a way for to allow more flexibility with implementation at the state and local level (Hill 2006). They allow states to cut across programs and eligibility requirements for appropriate services. In 2010, the State of Delaware combined three of its waiver programs: the elderly and disabled waiver, the assisted living waiver, and the brain injury waiver. This combination represented a shift away from the medical model to a functional model (Doneker, 2012). Previously, individuals had to choose among the waivers. For example, if an individual was on the assisted living waiver, but needed rehabilitation services from a stroke, he or she would not be able to access those services under the brain injury waiver without switching out of the assisted living waiver. The combined waivers allow caseworkers to operate using functional limitations to direct the services. This flexibility to select services from the larger menu increases the individual's choices and encourages a person-centered decision making process. The developmental disabilities (DD) waiver was not included in this change.

In Delaware, the Division of Services for Aging and Adults with Physical Disabilities initiated the Aging and Disability Resource Center (ADRC) to facilitate information dissemination and a coordinated process for aging individuals and AWDs to obtain services. With ADRC, a process of tracking families who have requested or utilized services through the division is underway. Individuals who access information or services are encouraged to call back if even a small change occurs. The division attempts to contact those families every 6–12 months to see how the individual and his or her caregiver are faring.

In addition, Delaware oversees three independent living centers in the state. The goal of the independent living centers is to provide information and advocacy to AWDs and their families. Their counselors work with the AWD and their family to create care plans and offer additional outreach activities including programming, training, and community social activities.

Common Issues in Planning

Professional attitudes toward definitions of family affect planning. While both aging and disabilities programs have recognized that families provide caregiving and protection for vulnerable family members, there are mixed approaches to including family members in long term planning. Lack of family involvement in comprehensive planning and lack of knowledge of how government programs and legal systems operate could result in their loved one losing needed supports, being placed in restrictive environment, or potentially be stripped of their many of their legal rights altogether (Heller & Caldwell, 2006).

Within developmental disabilities communities, there is controversy about focusing on the individual or the family. Increasing self-determination and consumer choice has been encouraged in the person-centered planning process (PCP). Although the great majority of AWDs live with their families, the family's participation in the decision making, planning, and implementing of plans has had less attention (Neely-Barnes, Graff, Marcenko, & Weber, 2008). Neely-Barnes and colleagues found four classes of involvement for families: highly involved, involved only in planning, involved only in financial, and uninvolved. The highly involved and planning only groups had more satisfaction with support services and the highly involved secured more services for the client and family. PCP emphasizes striking a balance between what the individual with the care needs wants, and what he or she needs, without limiting their thinking to the formal services available (O'Brien & O'Brien, 2006). PCP opens a dialog about the future and begins mobilizing resources by asking people involved in the individual's life regardless of varying definitions of family, what types of future support they can commit to providing, what resources they need to fulfill that commitment, and what outside services or resources are needed to fill in the gaps (O'Brien & O'Brien, 2006). Siblings are often involved in this process although parents sometimes are reluctant to discuss concrete expectations (Heller & Arnold, 2010). While 37% percent of parents indicated that a sibling would be responsible for care if the parent was no longer able and another 31% stated that they didn't know if the sibling would take on the caregiving role (EasterSeals, 2010)

PCP in adolescence and young adulthood has centered on the AWDs own preferences. According to Rubin and Nehring (2002), "self-determination suggests that it is the individuals with mental retardation and their families who should be determining what they need and should get" (p. 171). This approach assesses both the functional limitations of the impairment and the disability's effects on the person's interactions within the societal and family contexts. Contemporary perspectives on disability have advanced to accept disability as a part of the human experience (Silverstein, 2000). This perspective shifts the focus from trying to "fix" the individual to considering the socially constructed cultural and environmental factors that may be limiting the individual's ability to function and achieve a quality of life (Silverstein, 2000; World Health Organization, 2008).

In aging, the elders have also been central in planning, but recognition of caregivers and social support has included caregivers in discussions and, if they have a durable power of attorney in the area being discussed, are decision makers. Another aspect of oversight has been the state's role in protection against elder abuse and concern for the wellbeing of the individual. Some states have filial responsibility statutes and can seek financial support from adult children. Financial eligibility standards of Medicaid have also created difficulty for families when planning for long-term care making it difficulty for families to afford to provide care (Caro, 2006). Today, caregivers are important stakeholders in decisions about care and as a sounding board for concerns and questions to and from the professionals and the clients (Hubbard, Illingworth, Rowa-Dewar, Forbat, & Kearney, 2010).

The purpose of this study is to understand from the perspective of providers, caregivers and adults with disabilities, the family impact of current policies that dictate both eligibility and choice in support services for individuals and their families. The study focused on the perceptions of who is family in the context of caregiving and whether policies supported the function of caregiving. Perceptions of how the policies facilitated the maintenance of family ties and supported stronger relationships for diverse family forms are also discussed.

Rationale

The implementation of these policies, Home and Community-Based Services section 1915(c) of the Social Security Act, Money Follows the Person (MFP), and state level services for adults with mental health conditions has been met with similar difficulties in the State of Delaware. The Lewin consulting group was contracted by the state to study and report on the federal programs to support individuals with disabilities (Hertz, 2010). The focus of that study was a quantitative analysis of the cost factors and resource issues related to implementation. From this study, the Lewin group made several recommendations including continuation of the implementation and the consolidation of the service programs serving the needs of individuals with disabilities. While the state continued to review from a budgetary perspective the consolidation of services, a formal family impact analysis of the Delaware policies had not occurred.

Bogenschneider (2006) has been successful at forging a middle ground for policy makers to support the wellbeing of families in many critical areas. Her method of family impact analysis is the primary method used in family science. The family impact analysis method has been traditionally applied at the state level for federal policy. The family impact analysis method informed this case study of Delaware. This approach examined policy through the family lens and documented the competing interests between government programs, budgets, and service and provided a qualitative perspective beyond the quantitative analysis reported by the Lewin group.

A qualitative case study approach was chosen to obtain a greater understanding of the implementation of these programs at the state level. Prior studies have only been quantitative and fiscally focussed. This methodological approach provided the opportunity to illustrate the implementation of policy and its impact on individuals with disabilities and their family. The researcher placed the policies in context, geographically, demographically, socially, and historically within this framework.

Methods

Semi-structured interviews of key stakeholders, both in government and the community, were employed and available documents in the State of Delaware were reviewed. This qualitative case study data analysis relied on an insider's perception of the phenomenon being explored and implemented a case study approach. This family impact analysis included the perception of stakeholders, who are defined as individuals whom are influential in the writing or implementation of the policy, as well as consumers of the targeted programs (Bogenschneider, 2006).

Sample

In keeping with the case study research approach, a purposive sampling technique was used to identify the sample for this study (Creswell 1998). The State of Delaware has defined stakeholders for disability policy and services through its creation of the Governor's Commission on Community-Based Alternatives for Individuals with Disabilities and the State Council on Disabilities. These two bodies provided the starting ground for the sampling for this study. All members of the commission were invited for participation in this study. In addition, the departments, councils, and advocacy groups represented on the council were targeted separately. Several advocacy groups were identified by the prior study completed by the Lewin group and those groups were added to the study. The director/chair of each agency/department/council/non-profit was contacted for inclusion in the study. In the case when the director/ chair of the group was also identified as a member from the state council or the governor's commission, then that individual was asked to speak to both roles. Each director who participated was asked to identify up to three subcontractors, advisory council members, or state employees who that expert would identify as a stakeholder. The advocacy groups asked to participate in the study included those identified in the state review as well as those identified by the directors of the state agencies.

The advocacy groups included non-profit agencies. The chair/ director or their designee was asked to participate. Some agency participants were also consumers themselves, either directly or as a family member. When the contact from the advocacy group did not qualify as a consumer of the services from these federal programs, then that individual was asked to identify another individual from the group who is a consumer for inclusion in the study. Many representatives were also individuals with disabilities or caregivers themselves and served a dual role in this study.

This analysis in this chapter utilized a subset of the overall sample and included individuals specifically for their involvement in the provision of services and utilization of services for adults with physical disabilities, adults with developmental disabilities and aging adults, for their role as a caregiver or client. This group was appropriate to provide the opportunity to consider services from the perspective of individuals receiving services, caregivers for individuals receiving services and individuals implementing services and policy. The inclusion of both individuals with disabilities and aging adults provided the opportunity to consider how the definitions of family and the interpretation of the policies may be different in the disability versus aging fields.

The 24 participants were either employed in an agency or government office or were affiliated with the agencies for their work on a board or council. Nine of the participants were also either individuals with physical disabilities or family members of individuals with devel-

opmental disabilities. Three participants have provided care and coordinated care for an elderly family member. All but two were from northern
Delaware. Age and department/agency affiliation are not included as
these are immediate identifiers of the participants. Delaware is a small
state and concern for confidentiality and professional ethics have meant
that demographic information was not appropriate to use in the reporting
of the statements made.

Measures and Procedures

Qualitative data were collected through semi-structured interviews which provided organization to the interview, but also allowed the
questions to be modified, amended, or discarded as the inquiry continued (Daly, 2007). Identified respondents were contacted by phone or
e-mail with a full explanation of the study and asked to participate. Each
participant was interviewed one time for approximately one hour. Interviews took place in a public venue chosen by the participant. Interviews
followed a semi-structured format. Participants were asked questions regarding their perceptions of the family impact of the federal policies and
the effectiveness of implementation in the State of Delaware. The interviews were recorded and transcribed. Participants were not provided an
incentive to participate, however all participants received an executive
summary of the study. A qualitative case study approach facilitated rich
and in-depth descriptions, themes, and categories of information (Stake,
1995).

A qualitative case study includes extensive, rich text that draws
on multiple sources of information and is not limited to interviews. Observations, documents, and audio-visual materials are valuable sources of
data for this type of study (Creswell, 1998). Therefore, in addition to the
interviews, the data collection included a review of available e-materials,
website information, and policy information. Demographic information
and participation data was reviewed as available through the federal
reports on the State of Delaware.

The questions for the interview included the checklist for family impact analysis. This checklist has been extensively used in policy
analysis that evaluates the current policies and their impact on family
function in the four main areas of family formation, economic support,
childrearing, and family caregiving (Bogenschneider, 2006; Bogenschneider & Corbett, 2004). The analysis included examination of the process of
implementation. Consideration was given to the regulations, appropri-
ations, administrative practices, coordination with other programs, and
family-centered practices. The checklist for family impact analysis was
utilized (Bogenschneider, 2006). Participants were asked about their role
with the policies and their perceptions of the effectiveness of implementa-

tion in Delaware.

Data Analysis

The analysis for this study followed a case study approach (Stake, 1995). The interviews were recorded and transcribed. The content of the interviews were analyzed from a holistic perspective using a two-step process. The content was analyzed using direct interpretation of the case. The information regarding the process of accessing and receiving services was sequenced and the content was categorized based on the issues raised by participants, developing a thorough description of the case study. Categorical aggregation was used in the second step in the data analysis which allowed the compilation of instances until the data can be viewed as a class (Stake, 1995). This process resulted in a compilation and analysis of themes that were not dependent on the sequencing of events and facilitated the researcher's interpretations. The data analysis was a continuous and recursive process as each new emerging theme informed the researcher's interpretation and each piece of information was seen in the context previous information. Lincoln and Guba (1985) recommend this type of approach so that "lessons learned" during the analysis process are incorporated into the emergent design of the case.

While the advantage to a single case is that the goal is a rich, in-depth picture of the program/policy or event, the disadvantage is the lack of generalizability or ability to weigh the importance of the themes to larger populations (Creswell, 1998). For most qualitative researchers, generalizability is not the desired intent (Lincoln and Guba, 1985). In this study, the state of Delaware provided the initial boundary, the setting in time and historical context emerged from the inquiry process. This study may serve as a model for other states to proceed with an informed analysis of their own practices and for organizing and collecting data not currently available on program effectiveness.

All of the respondents in the study were asked to comment on their perception of the state's implementation of the waivers, and other state services. All respondents saw both strengths and challenges with the state's implementation. They shared stories of individuals who work in the agencies and service provider organizations. Many agency respondents discussed the recent efforts of these programs to address the needs of Delaware residents with disabilities.

Results: Process of Gaining Services

Respondents in the study began to tell a story of how the implementation of these services has impacted the individuals with disabilities and their families. According to the agency respondents, individuals with disabilities, and the family members, accessing services for an AWD

usually follow general steps in a process which was identified through
an open coding process. The first step involves becoming aware of the
services needed, what services may be available, and where to begin
exploring the possibilities. Transparency of the information and the
agency policies for implementation were key concerns. The significance
of individuals and their advocates having an "informed" advocate was
frequently mentioned. Once family members begin to gather information, their ability to connect to the appropriate services is influenced by
the label or type of disability for which they are seeking services. Issues
of equity arise in both the information and services available based on the
diagnosis. Obtaining the appropriate labels of the problems had a significant influence on a family's experience accessing services. The label, itself,
often shapes the process of assessing need at the individual, family, or
institutional level. The wrong label for a requested support service could
hamper getting services. For example, one agency may state that they do
not provide home health aids whereas if asked if they provide personal
attendants, the answer would be yes. From the perspective of the service recipient, there is little difference in the terms, but from the agency
perspective, there is a significant difference. Individuals and their advocates who are familiar with the labels and terms within the governmental
services, tend to receive more services and have an easier time accessing
those services.

Once eligibility is determined and assessment of need has been
completed, decisions must be made as to which services will be used.
At this point individuals and families are examining the level of risk
involved with each alternative of long-term care and deciding what risk
level will be acceptable to provide some independence. The concept of
risk had different meanings among both providers and clients. The areas
of family impact that have emerged for this paper involve the focus on
maintaining family ties, supporting family roles, and considering family
definitions as they are related to eligibility for different family structures.

Results: Family Impact

Maintaining Family Ties

The option to consider the needs and skills of the family was
noted by both the agency employees and the family members who participated in the study. From both the perception of the agency respondents and the family members, the implementation of state services does
not emphasize maintaining family ties. Most agency respondents, when
asked whether the services supported "maintaining family ties," stated that they had not thought of it in that way. According to an agency
participant, family support has been identified as a priority in the devel-

opmental disabilities community and the Delaware legislature passed the Family Support Services waiver to offer greater choice to individuals and families and require family education and training (www.dhss.delaware. gov/dhss/ddds/waiver.html). The participant explained that families are empowered to contract their own services and may consider services that are not covered under the Home and Community-based Services waivers such as respite, emergency temporary living arrangement, extended daycare, day habilitation, supported employment, and transportation. The family support services waiver would have provided a family assessment of need to the DD population; however, it has not been funded. In spite of the lack of funding, many participants explained that the Division of Developmental Disabilities Services and non-profit associations and service providers have attempted to provide wider services for family support. These services include, but are not limited to, respite care, family education on services and advocacy through workshops, and training programs. This effort was seen as supporting the family function of caregiving and acknowledging family ties.

Both respondents who worked in the DD field, and those who were family members of AWDs, believed that there was adequate acknowledgement of the family ties in the programs and services when the individuals with the developmental disability were children and youth. After 21, a shift in service provision policy occurs. The individual is provided adult services, often through the DD waiver, out of the family home. For example, an adult with DD can access a personal care aide to facilitate independent living in addition to day services and supported employment. Both agency respondents and family members agreed that to access the full spectrum of services, the individual must be living independently from his or her family members in an apartment or group home. For some families, this policy coincided with the family goals and needs. If the individual chooses to live with family and the family is interested in maintaining residential support for their family member, then the individual can access day services, but would not be able to access a personal care aide in the evening. In addition, the individual would not have the option to have a combination of a day program and/or supported employment. For example, a family and an individual had to choose between a day program and supported employment although they were trying to facilitate having a partial day program with several hours a day in supported employment. Family members and several agency employees believed that agency support for family responsibility was reduced if the family maintained a residential tie. One family member spoke of the "penalties" associated with choosing to have the adult child remain with the family members:

But as far as being at home and getting any services,

there is nothing. I mean if you have to buy a $45,000 van because your child is using a wheelchair there is no help for that. Families have no help as far as economic….you get your SSI check each month, she gets her SSI check and that's it, and she gets three hundred less than if I'd put her in a facility. If I put her in a facility or a nursing home for three months and pull her out, I would get Money Follows the Person, but I'm not willing to do that. I don't think agencies are pro-family. She would get more money each month, now it wouldn't be her money it would go to the facility for which…..you know, she wouldn't get as much money herself, but she would get a bigger check each month if she were in a facility. So the people in the facilities are getting, I believe, nine hundred and some dollars a month and she's getting six hundred and some dollars a month.

Family ties were not supported when caregivers needed more support. When the family member, who is caring for the adult with DD, is aging and needed greater support to provide for their adult child, the usual recommendation from the agencies is to transition that individual with DD into a group home so that the individual is settled into the new setting prior to the passing of his or her aging parents. One agency respondent and family member cited several professionals whom he worked with that articulated the process of adjustment in this way:

Here's the bind, and I'm thinking of a family… as I'm saying this because of them, [they] are in their eighties, and they won't move their son out. The bind is they die, there's no transition, all of sudden, you've got an emergency and a guy who has lived with them for fifty-seven years in this case, is now literally going to be plucked out of there and put over here; and the family has no way of helping with that transition because they're gone and you talk to pros in the field and most of them will say a smooth transition with the family helping with the transition is the way to go. And you can set it up any way you want. I said that too quickly, no you can't. But what families have done is okay, we're going to work with the DD folks and we want Johnny to go over here for a weekend and then come back and then we'll try another weekend and then come back and then we'll try a week and then come back. In other words, really transition it over a month or two.

The goal of this case was to move the adult child with a disability out of the home. Moving the son out of the family home did not support family ties or the aging parents' needs. When asked about the possibility of transitioning the individual while living with the aging parents by having aides come to the current place of residence to assist the individual in adjusting to other adults, the response was "that simply is not done." While it is possible for the family to leave or gift the family home to the adult child with a disability, there are legal and agency barriers. Families might stipulate in their will that their child can live in it indefinitely when the home is transferred to DDDS. According to the agency respondent, the division would have to make modifications to bring the house up to the code for a group home and then identify other individuals to occupy the home with the individual. Families would need to do research and work with a lawyer so the will and the trust can be facilitated and actually implemented. Information is not readily available from any of the state websites or providers for families to modify their home in advance of the death of the primary caregiver. One respondent explained:

> Only in the DD [community] folks have rarely done this,
> only if they can make it sensible financially because you
> leave the house to the individual, then you have to staff
> the house, now that's going to mean a provider, and the
> provider isn't going to want to staff a one-person house.
> So, you know, it's not realistic. It'll cost way too much and
> the DD folks aren't going to pay for that. So then you're
> going to have to bring other people into that home. Well
> you can't do that unless you set it before hand and there
> is another way to do it, which has been done, probably
> better to go through a provider. Set up the whole thing
> ahead of time. When we die, you know, we want this
> provider, they've agreed to come in if the state can put
> two more people in that home; so it's a home for three.
> Well the state won't do that; the provider won't do it, un-
> less the home is safe. So now you've got an architectural
> issue. You've got a million rules on what that home's got
> to have. How many homes do you know have a sprinkler
> system out there? Not many. That's number one and then
> you go from there. So before these people actually die,
> they should retrofit their house so that it could be used
> for persons with disabilities within the system. So the
> system's going to end up dictating what's got to be in that

house. So it's really complicated and that's why you don't see many people doing it.

Participants were not aware of any initiatives to make this process easier or more efficient so that families could see it as an option. In fact, the respondent quoted research that supports the idea of transitioning individuals out of their home. Some participants discussed that the families tend to avoid planning because they do not want to remove their adult child from their home and the community.

Aging parent caregivers may be less able to provide the evening care may require assistance for their own care. Several agency respondents and family members stated that they believe the various divisions could negotiate an agreement to provide assistance to the family, although the adult child is usually not eligible for an aide in the evening in a home setting. The family would have to come forward to advocate for this process or secure a case manager who is proactive in considering the "out of the box" solutions. Many agency respondents stated that it would be more likely that the caseworkers would recommend transition out of the family home for the adult with DD. Furthermore, the adult with DD may be providing some services to his/her parents that help these elderly parents avoid institutionalization for themselves. Several participants had not even considered any other option or been advised of the option. Another respondent explained:

> Right, exactly so what we do is we do try to educate
> people that if you try to address the needs as they occur,
> sometimes it doesn't really cost that much to really extend
> the length of the time that you can maintain someone.
> You know, now eventually they may need a lot of in-
> home care, but for starters it may not be all that bad, you
> know what I mean? Like you have someone come in for
> a couple hours a day, so for a couple hundred dollars a
> month, maybe we can help maintain them versus if you
> wait until it's a crisis and they have to go into a nursing
> home, you have to spend down everything. You know
> what I mean on that nursing home bill?

Another respondent dealt with aging issues:

> I would be able to maintain, it would be hard, it
> would be very hard; I mean I'm already looking into get-
> ting a lift, a ceiling lift to help us with that because we're
> aging; she's getting older and we have a lot.....but, I mean
> we have the shower that we've made floor to ceiling tiled

and then the thing in the middle, so we have an accessible
shower, we have her bedroom downstairs, we have pretty
much everything we need for her. We have the van, but
we've been able to do that, not every family's able to
do that. So that's why I think you have families that are
going to [facilities] when they're young. I mean I've had
families say to me, I don't know how much longer I'm going to be able to lift him and so I'm looking over at [a fa-
cility] to place him there and he's four years old. Because
they're afraid of the future that they're not going to have
the support and they're not going to be able to lift him

Most of the participants acknowledged a level of frustration in
finding appropriate options for services for families that have both needs
for services for an adult child with a disability and for the aging parent.
The definitions of family typically utilized in the policies and practices of
the agencies did not acknowledge the family's intergenerational family
structure. Solutions still emphasized institutions.

An adult accessing the HCBS waivers has an eligibility require-
ment that includes having no assets in his or her own name. Several
respondents discussed the concept of 'spending down' to gain eligibility.
In one individual's case, she inherited assets and rather than retaining
those assets, she was required to spend down the money immediately.
An agency administrator described spending down:

Like the system is to keep people under the Medicare.
In order to keep people spent down, they're buying big
screen TV's for the group homes or patio furniture for the
group homes... The things I used to have to approve to
get people spent down, is obscene. And a trust can't be set
up after the fact, once they have it; they can't....the federal
law won't allow it. You have to stay under the resource
and asset table.

Parents or other designees can maintain a "power of attorney"
and lend, rather than give economic support. Trusts are an option for
families but few families know about them. The inability to maintain
assets can influence the experience of family and limit the opportunity
to build community or fictive kin relationships. The individual may not
have the funds to support participation in activities or travel with extended family or friends. For families who want to maintain ties, some
agencies have found individual solutions. However, several respondents
noted that these solutions are not easy and they are not written into the

policies and depend on the skill of the professionals working on the case. One service provider described an example:

> I know in one case DDDS actually moved a family home because it was unsafe, the family didn't have any money and they found out that ten thousand dollars was cheaper than putting them in a group home which was a lot more expensive because the family's going to have to disperse and go someplace else to live. So what's happened is we have a very old model in this state and it's a model that if you get a group home, you get everything. If you live at home with mom and dad, you get a day club only. No transportation, you don't get support services...

Eligibility criterion for services are designed to prevent the expenditures going to less serious cases or being fraudulently allocated. This approach has led to families being forced to sever ties for individuals to have services. This practice was changed for children with disabilities in the 1980's, but lingers for adults with disabilities and for the aged who need nursing home care. It continues to be a major barrier to appropriate and cost effective solutions.

The Role of Family Support

Family support for the responsibility of caregiving was identified by many respondents as important to facilitate backup care as needed for the individual with a disability. The Division of Developmental Disabilities has continued to provide these services without the funded waiver; however, respondents state that the services need to be extended to more families. Such support would be beneficial for individuals with other types of disabilities and families with elderly members. Both the agency respondents and family members were in agreement that families and individuals with disabilities are not able to plan and troubleshoot because of a significant lack of back-up resources for times of crisis. One individual with a disability stated:

> The problem is many people don't have back-up and individuals who do can stay out of the institution. I am lucky that I have a lot of family support. One time I had to go for two months without my night-time aid. I was ready to get out of the hospital and none of my supports were ready. My friends and family did everything for me. They [case managers] wanted me to go to a facility. I knew it would be harder to get out once I went in.

Another participant stated:

> There were days when nobody showed up to come and take care of my mom while I went to work, and I would call the agency and oh well, you're just going to have to do without for the day …I know it goes on like with my friend who tells me these stories all the time, she ends up sleeping in her chair so many times, which is a health concern for her and anybody else who sleeps in their chair.

An individual with a disability described:

> Look it's someone's choice if they're told, hey look you know there's a chance that some health agency is going to like f-up the situation for the weekend, you might lay in bed, in your own feces and urine for the weekend by accident. It's that person's choice to still say, you know what, that beats living in this center. It's their choice…

Several agency respondents spoke of this same issue in the MFP program. Individuals with disabilities who are in institutions have already spent down and have few resources. In the absence of family, individuals in facilities have not built community connections or developed fictive kin relationships. Resources to support the vulnerable elderly and adults with disabilities are limited. Rules and regulations may alienate individuals from family care, support and advocacy. The ease with which services have facilitated separation individuals from family and community support has had many unintended consequences. One example of a consequence is the great difficulty of rebuilding a support system.

> Okay challenge was, well one of the biggest challenges is the state assumes there's going to be a family. You can't, I mean one of the things that used to drive me crazy at a few meetings is before the person gets out, and they have to provide their own back-up. You know family members, through family and/or friends, and …because normally people go into nursing homes and institutions because they don't have family…like is there some kind of magic pill that they take when they get out of the nursing home? So, they can all of sudden have all these family and friends to support them…

While individuals with disabilities need family support, family support must also be viewed through the lens of the family caregivers. Family caregivers need support. This difficulty in assessment is exacerbated by the aging process and the frequent changes in the caregivers' function that may require assessment by several agencies. Family support for the responsibility of caregiving was viewed as integral for maintaining the caregiving role and strong family relationships. Most participants identified this issue as it is described by one participant:

> Families need to have options, families need to have more support....we can't get kids out in the community or adults out in the community if we don't have transportation for them or you know we don't have the proper wheelchair for them to be in or they can't get a bath because they don't have the proper bath chair or the home isn't modified so they're not properly cared for, lack ability to visit, no one's using the universal design so you can't go visit, you know the aunt or the cousin or someone. Life if tough....life if tough for people with disabilities.

Another respondent discussed family support:

> I'm trying to think. Not formally, I don't think [there are any supports to help strengthen family ties and commitment]. I think families need respite and I think respite would help for families to be able to get away together once in a while or to be able to take your typical kids somewhere where they can have typical vacation, ...to be able to take the others and I am able to do that more than most people, but I can imagine it's a big problem in other families.

Families who lacked resources were referred to as "surviving" but in need of more support by several participants. A family member described:

> It's not typical so we may be asking way too much of families if they're working all day, they're a single mom, they're coming home, they have other kids, they're making dinner, and then in between they're supposed to.... their jobs may not be as flexible as mine. .. So, I don't think they look at....no, and I think I've seen many marriages break up because of the situation also; it's very hard on marriages. I have always said you either get close

or you get further apart. We did get closer, but there have
been some problems along the way, because it's very
tough, you know.

Another participant noted,

If the aging couple is getting to the point where they can't
care for themselves, you know families will, [you] probably know this, will go down trying, you know whether an
aging couple, … they will struggle until there is no more
struggle, and families of children, adult children with disabilities will do the same thing. They'll do whatever they
have to, to stay together. There's such great fear in letting
their children go to the system…

Family support was viewed by participants in two ways. Family
support was defined as immediate and extended family whom provide
direct caregiving to adults with disabilities. Having a support system allowed a higher quality of life for the AWDs. Family support also includes
services to family members to support their role in caregiving. Both types
of family support were viewed as needing greater attention in agency
services.

The Role of Definitions of Family and Risk in Eligibility
All of the participants recommended flexibility in the choices of
services available to families as ideal, but few saw it as a reality. Some
participants saw choices restricted by a diagnosis that guided family
decisions. Services were viewed as part of a frustrating rigid system. The
rules for eligibility did not acknowledge all family types. The rules for
services were not flexible. One individual with a disability shared this
story:

I don't necessarily look at services as being this big um-
brella thing. Although that is how a lot of the services
are offered. I may need or I may want just one service,
but it's very difficult to get that one service. You know,
we can give you all of these or we can give you none,
but we can't give you just that. Again, personal example,
when I first came to Delaware, I came to Delaware basi-
cally for school because I was accepted at College, and at
some point I didn't have any transportation when I came,
people told me, oh you know DAS [Division of Aging
Adults and Adults with Physical Disabilities] Oh, okay,

but I couldn't call DAS and just be put on. I had to be
referred by an agency at the time. Well I got in touch with
VR [Vocational Rehabilitation], but VR didn't want to do
anything because I didn't need any of their other services.
Well why don't you let us pay for school? Because I'm
up to here with loans and grants; I don't need you to pay
for school. But I had to become a client in order for them
to pay for transportation for me back and forth to school.
There's always a hoop you have to jump through.

Some individuals benefit when they know whom to ask, what to
ask for, and how to advocate in finding more flexibility. Most agency respondents identified flexibility of choices in services as a philosophy and
a goal, which is seldom achieved in the current service system. Choices
were limited by the structure of the waivers, such as rigid requirements
on the level of need. Choice and options for services were limited based
eligibility. Several participants discussed how family structure influenced
the eligibility process. For example, one participant had referred to his
wife throughout the interview and at a later point acknowledged that he
was not legally married. He stated:

I just say I'm married because we've been together so
long. I can't get married. If were to get married, I would
become her dependent. And then they would make her
my primary insurance provider or whatever insurance
she has. They'd say you need to go out and get a job and
provide insurance for him. And then, my Medicaid would
get ripped from me; it would get taken. So they have no
sensitivity or no thought of my beliefs or desire to be married. You know so I'm in this life that, you know, I guess
you could say just "shacking up."

Similarly, participants described families experiencing the onset
of a chronic illness of one spouse. One participant spoke of a relative that
was encouraged to divorce her husband so that he would be immediately eligible for Medicaid and she would not have to lose her life savings. While some rules exist to protect the family home for the surviving
spouse, the income and asset requirements require the individual to relin-
quish family ties to meet the eligibility and spend down requirements for
long term care through Medicaid. One respondent stated:

I know one of the down falls is that if you have a married
couple and they combine their incomes and they can't
afford the services outright on their own, but the husband

or the wife requires these in-home services, which they
can't afford…let's say she's working and he gets a disability check, with their combined incomes, they don't qualify
because they make too much money, but yet they can't
afford these services at home. My sister, her husband
is dying of Huntington's, and she was in that position
where they didn't have the income [level] because they
were married and the "State" said to her, divorce your
husband and we'll cover it.

This was a recurrent theme as another respondent notes:

I know people that are married, but when they get to a
point where they retire, and let's say they have to go into
an old age home to have the proper care. Because some
people eventually need 24 hour care… that cost will be
the responsibility of your spouse. So what are you going
to do, sell the house to pay for your spouse's care who is
in a nursing home? So, I know people that stay married
and they have jobs that they can get by on insurance …
they don't have the level of care that I have, but they stay
married and then when they hit like retirement, they're
going to get divorced to avoid giving away things…

One family's efforts to facilitate long-term care for the adult child
through commitments by several siblings were not supported by the
policies and practices of the state systems. The state would not consider a
sibling caring for a sibling with a disability as a family structure needing
a different approach to support services. This family was aware that if the
siblings take on residential support, then the individual would not receive as many services as she would if she went into a small group home.

Well we're very fortunate.…well we had talked to our
other children that at some point we would maybe put
her on the waiting list for the Center, it's not something
that we wanted to do, but you know we didn't want to
have to leave them with the burden, but they have all said
that no please don't put her on there, you know, one of us
will do it or we'll take turns but we will leave the house
to her, the house will be hers, and they will come in and
do whatever they need to do. So she has enough, she has
five brothers, so we're very fortunate in a lot of ways that
other families don't have.

Institutionalization relieves family members from direct caregiving, but this approach does not acknowledge the positive social and functional exchange that exists among family members. The family history of emotional and social exchange is ignored. Siblings may be better able to serve as caregivers if support services considered the needs of all family members and the family roles that each assumes.

Dignity of risk.

The concept of risk was a significant theme that rose from the data. Risk was referred to as the risk for harm. The agency respondents spoke about the fear that adults with disabilities and the elderly could be hurt or unable to get help while living on their own. While the agency respondents, individuals with disabilities, and the family members discussed issues of risk, many of them used the phrase "dignity of risk." One participant stated that "she reminds us every meeting of the dignity of risk," when referring to an administrator. This phrase was defined as an individual's right to decide how much risk he or she would like to accept. The term emphasizes that there is "dignity" in the choice to take on risk. However, how the risk was assessed and viewed varied among the respondent groups. According to the agency respondents, individuals working with the clients struggled with their own comfort level with the possible risks that the client is taking. The insistence on individuals having a backup plan is to ensure safety, however, when implementing a person-centered plan, that criteria serves as a barrier. According to one agency respondent, "people (individuals with disabilities) need family support, they need backup." The network of services relies on individuals having backup when the services are insufficient or falling short. For example, when an aide is unable to arrive, an individual needs to have a network of friends or family to be able to call. This articulated need for "back up" is an unwritten rule in the process for independent living. The Money Follows the Person program requires an individual have some level of backup or emergency support, and yet many of those in the institutions are in the institution because they did not have adequate family support or fictive kin. Several agency respondents articulated a paradox between the need for backup and safety and for allowing self-determination. One agency respondent stated, "We just keep repeating, 'an individual has a right to the dignity of risk'." However, agency respondents had different opinions as to when this becomes neglect or abuse.

From the perspective of both agency respondents and family members, family members may have a preference toward institutions due to a desire to ensure that the family member is safe and cared for at all times. When family members have power of attorney, they may be hesitant to consider community-based alternatives for their loved ones. This uneasiness was echoed in several interviews. Agency respondents attributed this to two different factors. The first is that the motives and needs of some families do not always match the motives and the desires of the individual. In discussing this, however, the agency respondents stated that they did not believe this was the most dominant issue. The second factor was that some families may not have a clear understanding of the potential and process for community-based services. Family members' perceptions of what level of risk is acceptable may be different from both the case manager and the individual receiving services.

Barriers to independence can also be seen through the medical evaluation process. Agency respondents spoke about the assessment of need and how, for the medical professionals assessing individuals, there may be a tendency toward being protective rather than allowing the individual to accept a level of risk. From a perspective of care, it indicates a personal apprehension and a feeling of personal risk. Many agency respondents acknowledged that while professionals may philosophically agree with the right of individuals to have the dignity of risk, they may also feel a sense of personal responsibility should the risk result in a negative consequence. This sense of personal responsibility may influence the assessments of medical evaluators and may result in an increase in barriers to independent living. Some agencies have worked diligently to address this conservative response. The MFP meeting minutes reflect extensive conversations about how to address issues of risk to facilitate the goals of individuals who wish to live in the community. In addition, there has been a top-down approach to training on self-determination and dignity of risk. The secretary of the Department of Health and Human Services spoke at length about efforts to educate and ensure that the message is sent to understand the rights of individuals regarding self-determination and risk. While self-determination is promoted, concerns were raised by several agency respondents and family members regarding consequences when something goes wrong. This disconnect was reflected in examples with individuals with developmental disabilities. When the individual is allowed to determine his or her diet, this could result in complications related to other health conditions such as diabetes. Several agency respondents stated that when that complication occurs there is a public push for accountability from the personnel involved in the case. One agency respondent stated, "Everyone is okay with an individual making the choice, but when something happens then the public wants someone to blame." The perception was that "someone is scapegoated" when a case goes wrong. This tendency toward blame is parallel to the experiences of case workers in the child welfare system (Pecora, 2006). Several individuals spoke about the success stories that have occurred when all the departments work together, but also identified that there is no specific process for how the departments work together.

The discussion of risk and family support is relevant when considering the needs of aging individuals. The desire for individuals to age in place was supported by most participants. Family support is met with more acceptances in families with aging family members. According to the agency respondents, families are doing more to assist aging members. However, several respondents said that families with aging members may be vulnerable to small changes in health. Advising families about risk may often result in underestimation of the individual's independent living risks. According to several agency respondents, individuals who have caseworkers need to have a reevaluation every six months. According to these same agency respondents, the issue of risk in families with an aging member influenced the level of choice for that person. Many respondents spoke about the families that do not want their loved one living on their own. They may feel more at ease and secure knowing that their family member is in a facility. In those cases, the family members themselves may be the barrier to self-determination.

Individuals with disabilities who participated in the study expressed strong views that the dignity of risk for individuals must be acknowledged. Several respondents spoke about how they accept risk so that they can live on their own. However, these same respondents acknowledged that many of the people they interface with perceive risk in different ways. One respondent spoke about how her family members had a different impression of what was an acceptable level of risk for her. From all the interviews, it is clear that risk is a negotiated concept that may hold different meanings for different people..

Discussion

The scope of this paper has centered on how the implementation of services for AWDs undercut or promote family and community ties. The horizons for both aging adults and individuals with disabilities have lengthened with greater medical technology and better caregiving. Integrating, adapting and collaborating service provision is crucial to successful outcomes.

The eligibility policies for the aging adults and adults with disabilities (AWD) are quite different in definitions of family and roles of family and allowable housing and home choices. Specific policies often define the family differently from the family's own perceptions and interactions. Legal definitions of family may proscribe service providers from recognizing the reality of families and may lead to denial of services. Being a member of a family may disqualify a client because of the pooled re-

sources of that family are above the policy criterion. Living at home with
a family member may disqualify a person with disabilities from some
support services. Requiring "independence" from family ties and homestead for eligibility for service of adults with disabilities has long term
consequences for more expensive and less responsive care. While institutional care has been rejected for children with disabilities, the professional
community assumes that smaller community based "homes" are appropriate for AWDs especially in young adult and elder life. In contrast,
much of the aging policy has focused on assisting aging in place, retrofitting homes to accommodate health needs and supplying in-home services. The major exception to supporting families with elders together has
been in the qualification for Medicaid nursing home care which requires
the person to have little resources. An analysis of perceptions of involvement by family members and the permeability of the family structure in
the definition of family should be recognized in programs.

Risk is often cited as a reason to require the AWD live in institutional settings. The acceptance of some risk for those aging in place
has become the norm for most elderly. Clinging to the mid-20th-century
notion that young adults need to be launched from the family early in
their 20's is dysfunctional for today's realities. This process may in fact
lead to institutionalization of three elders: parents and the AWD. Individuals who provide long-term care do not show higher levels of burden
and lower levels of health when they have feelings of reward and emotional wellbeing in the relationship. More could be done to acknowledge
individuals with developmental disabilities living with family as not only
an acceptable, but a positive family form. Family ties have provided a
positive quality of life, advocacy, and informal support services for many
years. The idea that the intergenerational relationship is less valuable and
less desirable than rather new, rather weak, peer relationships in community based institutions is inhibiting creative solutions. Reciprocity in the
exchange between the adult child with a disability and the aging parent
changes over time and may take many forms. The AWD may be an active
contributor to stabilizing aging parents. In addition, the emotional exchanges are often ignored when the individual with a disability makes
a transition out of the home. The concept of aging together is typical for
the elderly. Assisted living arrangements support couples living together.
Providing additional services in the home for the aging members also lifts
the burden felt by family members. This approach has not been applied
consistently to aging caregivers of adults with disabilities.

Current approaches do not consider assisting families with transitions within the current living arrangements in the community. The adult
child has lived in the community with their parent for an extended period
of time and may benefit from staying in that community once the parent

passes since he or she already has a social network there. Services could assist families with developing wills and other legal documents that help meet the state standards for care. Awareness and education about modifying the home for group living prior to the death of the parent(s) could be made available. Community-based services would recognize and value the individual with a disability having the opportunity to age in place and preserve family ties. While there may be a point when an institution setting is necessary, just as is common for elders, a cost-benefit analysis may reveal the excessive costs of prematurely placing a person in institutional settings.

Limitations

While this case study of the small State of Delaware cannot be generalized to every state or subunit within states directly, the issues raised are worthy of consideration and investigation by agencies as they attempt to use resources more effectively and improve the quality of life for these vulnerable people. Attention to how eligibility requirements affect families, long term planning and response to crises affect both the elderly and the AWD will be important everywhere. Restricted definitions of families' and individuals' rights to services should be reviewed. Replication of this work in other states could expand our understanding of the states as experimental agents shaping implementation and outcomes. This case study was done at a moment of great economic turmoil which is still not resolved. Follow up studies could also address whether waivers are sufficient for change or whether greater reform is needed. Other instruments for bringing together disabilities and aging professionals into closer contact and interchange could be helpful to facilitate better research programs and policy analysis.

Issues of race and gender were not directly addressed in the study. While questions on these topics were included, the participants did not see them as an issue. Further exploration of the intersectionality of race, gender and socioeconomic and disability status would add substantially to the knowledge in this area.

Implications and Recommendations

The integration of knowledge from the aging and disability literatures could enable better design of practices. Aging adults with an adult child with a disability may benefit from model services from both the aging and disability fields. State level policy analysis could provide better guidance to policy makers and program managers. Examining the theoretical frameworks and assumptions in addressing the aging of adults with disabilities and those of their parents and siblings who may be accumulating challenges themselves could suggest some further similarities and possible exchanges of perspectives and values between those fields and family science. Researchers should consider linking their research to include the total family in cost benefit analyses.

Including the total family in planning, making decisions about risk, and using of appropriate services could strengthen and provide a better quality of life for aging families with an AWD. Current disability policies have encouraged family dissolution, not resiliency in adult life. Finding new approaches to strengthen family and community ties could improve outcomes and reduce cost in the long run. Current practices offer more services to individuals with developmental disabilities who do not live with a family member; rewriting waivers may make change possible. The family caregivers may have provided a positive quality of life, advocacy, and informal support services for many years.

Agency employees may not be aware of their own assumptions and unexamined definitions of family and perceptions of risk. This lack of awareness may influence the client service process. Policies that seek to direct aid to those most in need have encouraged expensive institutional care over more years than may be necessary. Professional development that reframes thinking and approaches to incorporate diverse family structures could enable better practices and approaches to family support. The need for consistent processes and conversations to assess the level of risk associated with the options is also necessary. Opening the range of choices in long-term planning and respecting the family roles and definitions of relationships and options for the future will support the stability of family ties, the quality of life for all family members and the functions of family in caregiving.

Current policies encourage families to use family dissolution to become eligible for services. Some individuals are unable to consider marriage out of fear of losing services. Finally, family caregivers are struggling to maintain their roles. Available services may be able to facilitate this process by providing support to caregivers and families that may extend past the traditional services. Unique solutions to meeting family needs were highlighted in the stories from participants. Families need a system of support services that will offer a family assessment of need and will support new approaches to caregiving in diverse family structures.

References

Bengston, V., Lowenstein, A., Putney, N., & Gans, D. (2003). Global aging and challenges to families. In V. Bengtson, & A. Lowenstein (Eds.), *Global aging and challenges to families* (pp.1–26). New York: Aldine de Gruyter.

Bigby, C. (2004). But why are these questions being asked? Invited opinions and perspectives. *Journal of Intellectual and Developmental Disabilities, 29,* 202–205.

Bogenschneider, K. (2006). *Family policy matters: How policymaking affects families and what professionals can do.* Hillsdale, NJ: Lawrence Erlbaum Associates.

Braddock, D., Hemp, R. & Rizzolo, M. C. (2008). *The state of the states in developmental disabilities.* Washington, DC: American Association on Intellectual and Developmental Disabilities.

Butler, R. N. (2008). *The longevity revolution: The benefits and challenges of living a long life.* NY: Public Affairs.

Caro, F. G. (2006). Family aging policy: Introduction. In F. G. Caro (ed.). *Family and aging policy* (1-5). NY: Haworth Press.

Cherlin, A. J. (2010, June). Demographic trends in the United States. *Journal of Marriage and Family* 72(3), 403-419. doi: 10.1111/j.1741-3737.2010.00710.x

Creswell, J. (1998). *Qualitative inquiry and research design: Choosing among five traditions.* Thousand Oaks, CA: Sage.

Doneker, K. L. (2012). Caregiving of aging adults and adults with disabilities: Theoretical foundations and policy alternatives. Proquest Dissertations.

Easterseals. (2010). *Easterseals Living with a Disability Study.* Chicago, IL: Mass Mutual.

Freedman, R., Krauss, M., & Seltzer, M. (1997). Aging parent's residential plans for adults with mental retardation. *Mental Retardation, 35,* 114–123.

Feinberg, L. F., Horvath, J., Hunt, G., & Plosster, L. (2003). Family caregiving and public policy principles for change. National Alliance on Family Caregiving. Retrieved from http://www.caregiving.org/data/principles04.pdf.

Harootyan, R. A., & Bengston, V. (1994). Intergenerational linkages: The context of the study. In R. A. Harootyan, & V. Bengston (Eds.), *Intergenerational linkages: Hidden connections in American society* (pp. 1–16). New York: Springer.

Harrington, C., Chapman, S., & Miller, E. (2005). Trends in the supply of long-term care facilities and beds in the United States. *Journal of Applied Gerontology, 24,* 265–282.

Heller, T., & Arnold, C. K. (2010). Siblings of adults with developmental disabilities: Psychosocial outcomes, relationships, and future planning. *Journal of Policy and Practice in Intellectual Disabilities, 7,* 16–25.

Heller, T., & Caldwell, J. (2006). Supporting aging caregivers and adults with developmental disabilities in future planning. *Mental Retardation, 44,* 189–202.

Hill, G. J. (2006). State policy decisions in the 1990's: Implications for the financial well being of later life families. In F. G. Caro (ed.). *Family and aging policy.* NY: Haworth Press, pp. 211-227.

Hubbard, G., Illingworth, N., Rowa-Dewar, N., Forbat, L., & Kearney, N. (2010). Treatment decision-making in cancer care: The role of the career. *Journal of Clinical Nursing 19,* 2023–2031.

Irvin, C., Lipson, D., Simon, S., Wenzlow, A., & Ballou, J. (2010). Money follows the person 2009 annual evaluation report. Mathematica Policy Research, Inc. Retrieved from http://www.mathematica-mpr.com/publications/PDFs/health/MFP_2009_Annual.pdf

Levine, P., & Wagner, M. (2007). Transition experiences of young adults who received special education services as adolescents. In W. Osgood, M. Foster, C. Flanagan & G. Ruth (Eds.), *On your own without a net: The transition to adulthood for vulnerable populations* (pp. 202–238). Chicago, IL: University of Chicago Press.

Liebig, P. S., Koenig,T., & Pynoos, J. (2006). Zoning, accessory dwelling units and family caregiving. In F. G. Caro (ed.). *Family and aging policy* (pp. 155-172).NY: Haworth Press.

Levine, P., & Wagner, M. (2007). Transition experiences of young adults who received special education services as adolescents. In W. Osgood, M. Foster, C. Flanagan & G. Ruth (Eds.), *On your own without a net: The transition to adulthood for vulnerable populations* (pp. 202–238). Chicago, IL: University of Chicago Press.

Lowenstein, A., & Bengtson, V. (2003). Challenges of global aging to families in the 21st century. In V. Bengtson & A. Lowenstein (Eds.), *Global aging and challenges to families* (pp. 371–377). New York: Aldine de Gruyter.

Moody, H. R. (2006). *Aging: Concepts & controversies* (10th ed.). Thousand Oaks, CA: Pine Forge Press.

Mulvany, F., Barron, S., & McConkey, R. (2007). Residential provision for adult persons with intellectual disabilities in Ireland. *Journal of Applied Research in Intellectual Disabilities, 20,* 70–76.

Neely-Barnes, S., Graff, J. C., Marcenko, M., & Weber, L. (2008). Family decision making: Benefits to person with developmental disabilities and their family members. *Intellectual and Developmental Disabilities 46*(2) 93–105.

O'Brien, C. L., & O'Brien, J. (2006). The origins of person-centered planning. In S. H. Holburn, & P. M. Vietze (Eds.), *Person-centered planning: Research practice and future directions* (pp. 1–27). Baltimore, MD: Brookes Publishing.

Pecora, P. (2006). Child welfare policies and programs. In J. Jenson, & M. Fraser (Eds.), *Social policy for children and families* (pp. 19–66). Thousand Oaks, CA: Sage.

Ploeg, J., Campbell, L., Denton, M., Joshi, A., & Davies, S. (2003, March 31). Helping to build and rebuild secure lives and futures: Financial transfers from parents to adult children and grandchildren. *Canadian Journal on Aging Supplement,* S113–125.

Price, C. A. & Humble, A. M. (2010). Stress and coping in later life. In S.J. Price, C. A. Price & P.C. McKenry, Eds. *Families & change: Coping with stressful events and transitions.* Los Angeles, CA: Sage pp. 51-72.

Rubin, L. & Nehring, W. (2002). From medical model to integrated health care delivery: AAMR medicine and nursing initiatives from 1975-1999. In R. Schalock, P. Baker, & D. Croser (Eds.), *Embarking on a new century; Mental retardation at the end of the 20th century* (pp. 167-181). Washington, DC: American Association of Mental Retardation.

Settles, B. H. (2007, May). *Navigating private and public care systems: Whose responsibilities? Which style?* Committee on Family Research, International Sociological Association, Toronto, Canada.

Silverstein, M. & Giarrusso, R. (2010). Aging and family life. *Journal of Marriage and Family 72*(5). pp. 1039-1058. doi:10.1111/j1741-3737.2010.00749.x

Silverstein, R. (2000). An overview of the emerging disability policy framework: A guidepost for analyzing public policy. *Iowa Law Review, 85* (1), 757.

Stake, R.E. (1995). *The Art of the Case Study.* Thousand Oaks, CA: Sage.

Stepler, R. (2016). *Smaller Share of Women Ages 65 and Older are Living Alone: More are Living with Spouse and Children.* Washington, D.C.: Pew Research Center.

Taylor, S.J. (2004). Caught in the continuum: A critical analysis of the principle of the least restrictive environment. *Research & Practice for Persons with Severe Disabilities, 29*(4), 218-230.

U.S. Department of Housing and Urban Development (2017). Disability rights in housing. Retrieved from https://portal.hud.gov/hud-portal/HUD?src=/program_offices/fair_housing_equal_opp/disabilities/inhousing

Weeks, L. E., Nilsson, T., Bryanton, O., & Kozma, A. (2009). Current and future concerns of older parents of sons and daughters with intellectual disabilities. *Journal of Policy and Practice in Intellectual Disabilities, 6,* 180-188.

World Health Organization (WHO), Commission on Determinants of Health. (2008). *Closing the gap in a generation: Health equity through action on the determinants of health.* Final report. Geneva, Switzerland: WHO.

Chapter Two

**Exploring a Policy of Displacement Related to
Adults with Intellectual and Developmental Disabilities**

Katrina Powell

Alexis Priestley

Katherine Randall

Pamela Teaster

Anisa Zvonkovic

Virginia Tech

In Virginia, several large residential centers for persons with intellectual and developmental disabilities (ID/DD) are in various phases of closing. As a result of a 2012 settlement agreement between the Commonwealth of Virginia and the U.S. Department of Justice, several thousand residents of the Virginia Training Centers will be relocated to smaller group homes and community living through phased closures by 2020. This chapter provides a historical overview of the Centers in the state and the implications for these closures, not only for Virginia residents and their families but also for other states facing similar judgements. In addition, we describe our approach to understanding how the process of displacement affects the health and well-being of a population of highly vulnerable and medically fragile residents residing in four of the five VTCs anticipating closure within the next four years.

Previous research has explored overall outcomes of relocating persons with ID/DD into community settings (Bekhet & Zauszniewski 2014; Barber, Cooper & Owen, 1994). However, researchers have defined the ID/DD population in general terms and have explored neither the particular needs of these residents or nor the complex family and system dynamics involved in their care prior to, during, or post-move. This chapter, therefore, addresses the family decision-making processes involved in finding alternative care while facing complex financial, geographical, and familial factors.

Though individuals with profound medical and physical conditions constitute a small portion of the ID/DD population, they are the most vulnerable residents, and consequently, are the most difficult to relocate. The soon-to-be-displaced residents' experiences of displacement are often mediated through their family members, paid caregivers, and communities as well as through power dynamics between the residents and the power structures in which they live. As we provide information about our preliminary data collection and analysis, we suggest ways that our research stands to inform policy and procedures used when a forced displacement of a highly vulnerable population occurs.

History of the Virginia Training Centers

Since the opening of its first facility in 1910, the Commonwealth of Virginia has sponsored live-in medical residences for persons with ID/DD. Now known as training centers (TCs), these facilities currently provide occupational, speech, and physical therapies; 24/7 medical care; and support in activities of daily living (ADLs) provided by qualified residential services staff ("Services," 2016).

As of 2013, 4.8% of those served by Virginia's Developmental Disability System were living in TCs (Stewart, 2013). For these few thousand Virginians, the TCs have been, and were intended to be, their homes for most of their lives. However, the idea of a total institution (Goffman, 1968) is no longer deemed appropriate by the legal system nor by prevailing attitudes toward individuals with disabilities (Welshman & Walmsley, 2006), a situation that has put the TCs in an uncomfortable spotlight. When the state of Virginia was adjudged out of compliance with the *Olmstead* decision (2010), state-level conversations began about how to secure the necessary funding to accommodate individuals with ID/DD who desired expanded community integration. The state offers Medicaid waivers for persons with ID/DD to access the variety of services that they need; however, as of March 2015, 7,830 people were on the waiting list for such services, with nearly 4,800 deemed in need of "urgent" care (Daily Press, 2015). Advocates for the Centers' closing argue that the money saved by closing and selling the Center properties will fund more waivers, as the cost of care in a community setting is arguably cheaper than care in an institution. "We just simply cannot afford to run two systems simultaneously," said State Health and Human Resources Secretary Bill Hazel to the Associated Press. "We have to choose. We are choosing the one we believe individuals want" (Potter, 2012).

Central Virginia Training Center

Beyond financial concerns, the historical context of the TCs — more specifically, the Central Virginia Training Center in Lynchburg, Virginia—leaves open an uncomfortable door that the state may be happy to shut. In 1927, the Virginia State Colony for Epileptics and Feebleminded, as the TC was then known, became infamous for housing Carrie Buck, the plaintiff in a landmark Supreme Court case permitting forced sterilizations of those deemed "mental defectives with cacogenic potentialities." From 1927 until 1979, over 7,000 individuals were sterilized across the state of Virginia (Currell & Cogdell, 2006; Dorr, 2006; Lombardo, 2008). In a discussion of *Buck v. Bell*, Powell (2015) wrote:

> U.S. Supreme Court Justice Oliver Wendell Holmes stated in his majority opinion that 'three generations of imbeciles is enough,' reflecting the ubiquity of eugenics discourses in the U.S. at that time, and using the label 'imbecile' to describe Carrie Buck's mental abilities. The poor were often deemed feeble-minded merely because they lived outside social norms. As a result, they were marked as abject and the rationale was to institutionalize them. (46)

As cultural attitudes have progressed, there has been increased awareness of and discomfort around the recognition of the rights of those marginalized for being "outside social norms." Those with ID/DD often fall into this category. In the minds of many—including those of the courts—the continued operation of facilities such as the TC perpetuates an unfortunate and dangerous legacy of discrimination and neglect.

Established in 1910, the facility was originally intended to house people with epilepsy who had previously been living in Virginia's three state mental hospitals. The expansion to include "feebleminded" women occurred in 1913, so that in 1919, the Colony housed approximately 500 residents. By 1940, the facility name changed to the Lynchburg State Colony, which housed just over 2,000 residents. In the 1950s, a national push to develop training programs for those with mental disabilities led to increased staff skills in patient care and teaching, and by 1955, a majority of Colony residents were being trained in life skills. That same year, "The Colony," was renamed the Lynchburg Training School and Hospital. Due to demand, a second facility—the Southside Virginia Training Center—opened in Petersburg, Virginia in 1971, followed closely by the opening of the Northern Virginia Training Center (1973), the Southeastern Virginia Training Center (1975), and the Southwestern Virginia Training Center (1976).

Over time, the state made efforts to shift the mission and purpose of the TCs. For example, since 2005,[1] each Center has a Human Rights

---

[1] See http://www.dbhds.virginia.gov/individuals-and-families/human-rights/

Advocate that reports directly to the Virginia Department of Behavioral Health and Developmental Services. As the website of the Southeastern Virginia Training Center describes,

> [t]here has also been a transition from a focus on reme-
> diation of skill deficits and program matching people to
> programs, to an emphasis on strengths and the adaptation
> of environments to support the interests and abilities of
> individuals. The impetus for this change has largely come
> from the individuals for whom we have been providing
> services. Individuals with disabilities do not consider
> themselves to be "broken" or in need of being "fixed".
> Rather, they seek to live their lives in ways that are con-
> sistent with their own interests, preferences, and aspira-
> tions.[2]

As cultural attitudes have progressed, there has been increased awareness of and discomfort around the recognition of the rights of those marginalized, including those with ID/DD. In the minds of many—including those of the courts—the continued operation of facilities such as the TCs perpetuates an unfortunate and dangerous legacy of discrimination and neglect by state institutions.

The *Olmstead* Decision

The contemporary attitude towards institutionalization is reflected in the *Olmstead* ruling (1999), a landmark case that changed legal and rhetorical positioning for persons with ID/DD (Caley & Caley, 2010; National Council on Disability, 2010; Nielson, 2012; Snyder-Hegener, 2010; Rosenbaum & Teitelbaum, 2004; Stefan, 2010; Toland, 2008; Trent, 2006; Zendell, 2007). The Supreme Court was asked to elucidate specific language from the Americans with Disabilities Act of 1990 (ADA), which prohibits discrimination based on mental or physical disability, and further described "the isolation and segregation of individuals with disabilities as a serious and pervasive form of discrimination" (*Olmstead v. L.C.*, 1999). In adjudicating the *Olmstead* decision, the Supreme Court concurred that "institutional placement of persons who can handle and benefit from community settings perpetuates unwarranted assumptions that persons so isolated are incapable or unworthy of participating

---

local-hr-committees for information about the development of human rights committees in the Commonwealth of Virginia.
[2] Retrieved from http://www.sevtc.dbhds.virginia.gov/. The websites for the TCs have been removed or left inactive as they have closed, but the SEVTC website is current.

in community life." This decision further clarified Title II of the ADA, which requires both local and state governments to "administer services, programs, and activities in the most integrated setting appropriate to the needs of qualified individuals with disabilities," also known as the Integration Mandate. The Court further specified three criteria that must be met in order to warrant transferring institutionalized persons to more integrated settings:

> [W]hen the State's treatment professionals have deter-
> mined that community placement is appropriate, the
> transfer from institutional care to a less restrictive set-
> ting is not opposed by the affected individual, and the
> placement can be reasonably accommodated, taking into
> account the resources available to the State and the needs
> of others with mental disabilities.

The Central Virginia Training Center was first investigated by the U.S. Attorney General's office in 2008 regarding the Civil Rights of Institutionalized Persons Act. This investigation was expanded to include the Americans with Disabilities Act (ADA) and *Olmstead* compliance in 2010. In February of 2011, the US Attorney General's office issued a Findings Letter to then Governor of Virginia, Bob McDonnell, notifying him of Virginia's noncompliance with the ADA. Citing Virginia's "systematic failures" which cause "unnecessary institutionalization," and place "individuals currently in the community at risk of unnecessary institutionalization", the Findings Letter highlights three primary causes of Virginia's noncompliance: "a lack of services in the community, particularly for individuals with complex needs, and a slow and muddled discharge and transition planning process" (Perez, 2011).

In January of 2012, the United States simultaneously filed both a Complaint and a Settlement Agreement that addressed the three areas of concern. The main goals of the settlement were to prevent unnecessary institutionalization and ensure that those who currently reside in institutions "have a meaningful opportunity to receive services that meet their needs in the community" (U.S. v. Commonwealth of Virginia, 2012). In order to meet these goals, Virginia agreed to increase community-based services, primarily through increasing family supports, enhancing Medicaid waivers, and expanding and enhancing crisis and employment services.[3]

Since December 2012, an Independent Reviewer has been periodically assessing Virginia's work towards compliance with the Settlement

[3] Summary of Settlement Agreement in *United States v. Commonwealth of Virginia.* (2012 March 7). Retrieved from https://www.justice.gov/sites/default/files/crt/legacy/2012/03/15/va-ada_settlementsumm_3-7-12.pdf

Agreement. In the first report, the Independent Reviewer writes that when Virginia has fully implemented the Agreement, there will be at least 4170 individuals "supported with integrated residential and day services in the community", including 805 people who, as of 2012, live in the five TCs across Virginia. Subsequent reports found that Virginia struggled to effectively restructure its Home and Community Based Services (HCBS) waivers, which are a major component of the state's plan to come into compliance with the Settlement Agreement. While the state initially exceeded the number of waivers required by the Agreement, the kinds of available supports and services those waivers allowed were not meeting the "most integrated settings possible" proviso (Fletcher, 2013). However, in early September 2016, Virginia successfully launched a redesigned waiver program, which included a more streamlined application process, a wider variety of community-based services, and additional, less expensive services that were previously harder to acquire, like wheelchair ramps and backyard fences (Kleiner, 2016).

Implications for Other States

Virginia is not the only state to have struggled meeting the standards of the Olmstead Act — and the Integration Mandate. Across the country, at least eighteen other cases that involve violations of the Olmstead Act are currently in litigation or have been settled. Additional cases are pending in Mississippi, Washington, D.C., New Jersey, Pennsylvania, and Connecticut, all of which specifically reference language from the Integration Mandate as grounds for legal action against public and private institutions in these states.

For the most part, the cases that have been settled are found in favor of the United States. There are, however, a few notable cases where reaching a settlement has been more complicated. In the case of *Benjamin v. Dept. Pub. Welfare*, which was filed against the state of Pennsylvania in 2010, the Court ruled that the Defendants, by keeping persons with developmental disabilities in large, public institutions, were in violation of Title II of the ADA. However, subsequent to the Court's order, a group of individuals currently living in these institutions, referred to collectively as "Springstead," appealed the decision, citing their right "to protect their ability to continue to live in a State Center" (Benjamin v. Department of Public Welfare, 2009). Late in 2012, the Third Circuit court ruled in favor of this group of individuals, finding that because these individuals are stakeholders in the settlement agreement, they should have been, but were not, adequately represented during the initial lawsuit. The case is currently in the district court in the state of Pennsylvania.

Pending Litigation

While the *United States v. Commonwealth of Virginia* case has been settled, several other states currently face similar litigation. Mississippi, New Jersey, Connecticut, the District of Columbia, South Dakota, Pennsylvania, and Texas are all in various stages of the litigation process. In all cases, the same language from the Integration Mandate in the Olmstead Act is cited: "[services must be provided] in the most integrated setting appropriate to the needs of qualified individuals with disabilities" (*Olmstead v. L.C., 1999*). Consequently, we posit that while our findings are specific to the Virginia Training Centers, the broader implications of our results could impact both Settlement Agreements in states facing similar ADA compliance issues and individual institutions that seek to better understand the needs of its residents during resettlement processes. In terms of policymaking and policy implementation, we address the impacts of policy that have unintended consequences. To explain, policy changes such as the imminent TC closures have been enacted for the public good: a body of evidence suggests that closures of institutions that relocate residents into community living has benefitted many people (Patti et.al., 2010). Studies that examine relocations of vulnerable populations focus on higher functioning persons who are capable of living relatively independent lives (Barber et al., 1994; Cooper & Picton, 2000; Patti et al., 2010; Young et al., 1998). Further, most studies focus on a part of the ID/DD population for whom the transition is specifically designed (e.g., Patti, et al., 2010 study of individuals with Down Syndrome). Several studies suggest that many people with ID/DD respond well to community living after a period of adjustment (Allen, 2001; Bekhet & Zauszniewski, 2014; Cooper & Picton, 2000). Davis et al. (2000) report the results of relocation among states that have been successful in closing institutions and providing community-based living for persons with ID. However, because some of the institutionalized population in Virginia feels as if its voice has been neglected in these court decisions, our goal is to spotlight testimonies from patients and families who, as described in the above decision, have not been "adequately represented."

Justification of The Study

Only a few studies (Allen, 2001; Bekhet & Zauszniewski, 2014; Cooper & Picton, 2001) focus on the transition of residents with profound disabilities requiring 24/7 medical care and their transition into smaller residential homes. Despite significant changes in the approach to care at the TCs, DOJ's findings and the state's decision to close alters the approach to care to from large, multiservice campus settings to small group home settings. Moreover, by stressing the individual outcomes of new placements, studies have disregarded the important aspects of community and sense of place that may have existed in TCs (Kozma, A., Mansell, J., & Beadle-Brown, J., 2009; Lakin, K.C., Prouty, R., Polister, B., & Coucouvants, K., 2003; Larson, S.A., Salmi, P., Smith, D., Anderson, L., & Hewitt, A.S., 2013; Lorde and Hearn, 1987; Woodman, A.C., Mailick, M.R., Anderson, K.A., & Esbensen, A.J. (2014).

Profound physical and medical limitations of this vulnerable and medically fragile population of adults make it difficult to place and provide appropriate services in the community. The expensive medical equipment and other therapies are unavailable in most group homes. Lack of access to equipment and therapies may limit how much residents can interact with each other and with their new communities.

Our research considers the situation of VTC residents as similar to the experiences of other individuals who have been displaced from their homes. A goal of our project is to illuminate the hidden nature of the displacement of vulnerable and medically fragile persons, a displacement for which many residents and families must navigate the displacement and its effects. Facility closures that are the result of state and federal policy are not typically viewed as disasters. However, residents of the TCs may well experience their displacement in similar ways to communities displaced due to natural disaster or civil unrest, albeit on a smaller scale. Because displacement health impacts are common in a variety of displacement events (Oliver-Smith, 2010; Powell 2015; Baines 2004), our investigation of the closures of the VTCs examines displacement trajectories of focal residents, their families, paid caregivers, and affected communities. Our investigation: (1) highlights the effects of displacement and how the identities of the residents and families are reshaped by their interactions, including those with paid caregivers and the larger community; (2) traces the implications of the displacement experience for the focal residents' health and well-being, and (3) suggests how to mitigate its impacts upon those who may be displaced by future events.

Theoretical Grounding

Because *process* is a significant factor in adapting to a displacement event, we employed a Bronfenbrennerian socioecological perspective upon the transitions of focal residents and the larger systems around them, incorporating the newest framing of this perspective that includes the notion of change over time (the chronosystem) with a renewed focus on interpersonal process and individual characteristics. This framing positions focal residents in terms of their ontological age, their condition, their time in the TCs, the nature of the linked lives between the residents and their family members (family life course perspective and family as a microsystem), and the linkages between the residents and their paid care-givers. The socioecological perspective further frames the transitioning individual into nested systems, including family members and systems around them, as well as changes in their communities, resources, and policies. Note that mesosystems are seen as important linkages between different microsystems, and as such, the connections between family members and residential settings are illustrated. The stronger those connections and the more consistent the structured processes of behavior and experiences between them, the better for development. Figure 1 demonstrates our application of the theoretical model.

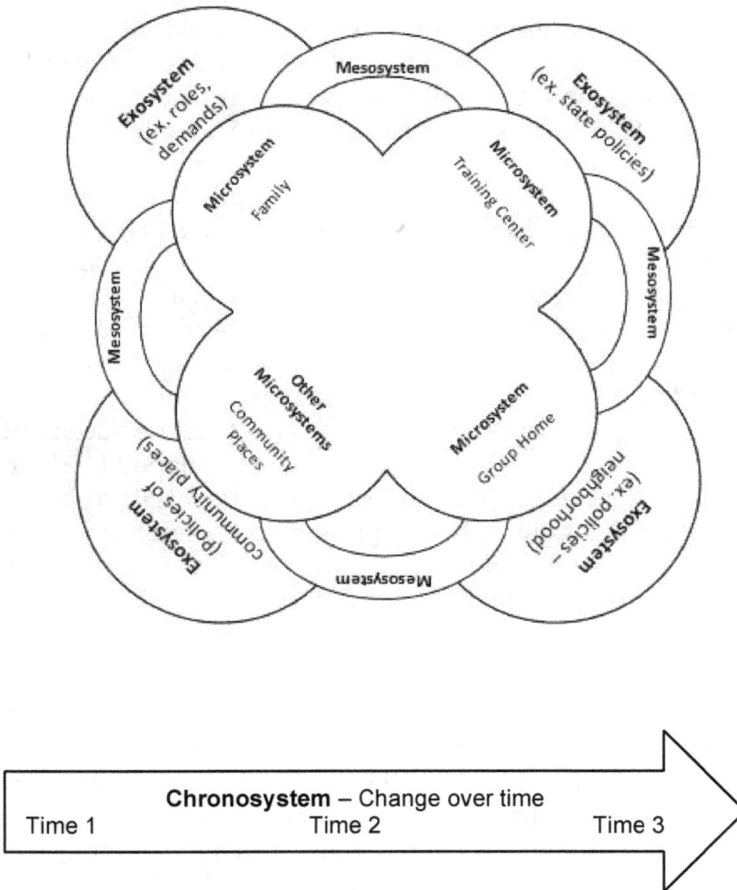

Figure 1. Socioecological Framework.

Incorporation of the elements of person, process, and context facilitates pairing this perspective with a rhetorical lens that focuses on understandings of identity as a key lens. The emphasis on process from the Bronfenbrenner model allows exploration of identity representations of key family members, because identities are constituted and reconstituted through the specific interactions individuals have with others. These identities are important drivers of the ways family members involve themselves in residential transitions for the focal residents. The approach, guided by rhetorical analysis of identity and the socioecological perspective, enhances the theoretical rigor of the study and thus increases the impact of its results.

Methodology

We conducted a feasibility study in the fall of 2015 with 20 families of TC residents who were slated to be moved. Using individual residents as the focal point, our sampling frame involved interviewing the focal resident, at least one family member, and a paid caregiver of the resident. All but one of the focal residents were male. Fifteen of the family members were parents; in two cases, both the mother and father or mother and stepfather were interviewed. In cases in which parents were deceased, siblings were interviewed. In two cases, multiple siblings from the same family were interviewed. We established collaborative working relationships with parent groups, TC staff, and community service groups involved in monitoring the transition and new placements.

Interviews were conducted in person, or by telephone or video-conference and were between 30-60 minutes in duration. After face to face meetings of residents in their homes at the TCs, we discovered that the remaining residents were difficult to place and nonverbal and/or medically fragile. We understood more about how paid caregivers were central to the residents' lives and to our inquiry. The paid caregivers facilitated communication with the residents, were knowledgeable about residents' attitudes related to the transition, and were involved in discharge planning.

In addition to asking residents and family members about their well-being during and after the transition, we also asked the caregiver about the resident's adjustment to the transition. For our study, both family members and staff members at TCs (paid caregivers and administrators) commented on ways that the move was affecting the residents. Effects included the disruption of routines caused by the moves of other residents, increased agitation, and missing friends and caregivers who had already resigned in order to find other work.

We determined that interviews were most fruitful at about three months pre-move, when care plans were being constructed and group home placements were being finalized, as opposed to six months or a year pre-move, when transition planning had barely commenced. This scope allowed us to gather data most relevant to how focal residents, their family members, and caretakers were affected by the beginning of the transition process. We conducted interviews among residents of three TCs in three disparate locations: the Northern Virginia Training Center (suburban Washington, DC); the Southwest Virginia Training Center (rural Hillsville, Virginia); and the Central Virginia Training Center (problematic history was described in detail previously), in Lynchburg Virginia. Each location had assets and challenges in terms of finding appropriate placements for residents. Family members residing in near the TCs tended to have different educational levels and unique assets and challenges germane to the geographic location. Based on our preliminary findings, we determined that the focal resident's health and well-being, family members, paid caregivers, and interaction with community stake-holders, significantly affect and are affected by the transition.

Analytic Strategy

Our analytic strategy was guided by the categories suggested by our Bronfenbrennerian model: the individual level of the focal resident, the family, the process of how the family member and the resident nego-tiated with the systems that affected them, related to the transition out of the TC, going to the broader levels of the community and the larger policy level. Examples of information that fit within each level are listed in Table 1.

In order to analyze the interview data, based on our theoretical approaches incorporating displacement, the socioecological framework, and family life course perspectives, we use standard methods of quali-tative analysis focusing on ways that residents families, paid caregivers, and community stakeholders represented and narrated their experiences of displacement (Ragin, Nagel & White; Gerring; Roy et al.). Data analy-sis began with the theoretically-derived categories (Gilgun, 2005; Glaser & Strauss, 1967), a technique developed by Hsieh and Shannon (2005) as directed content analysis and identified by Gilgun (2005) as deductive qualitative analysis. This method allows for a "starting point" on complex data (*juxta vivo* or linked to concepts from the literature, LaRossa, 2012; Swenson, Zvonkovic, Rojas-McWhinney, & Gerst, 2015). Categories from the Bronfenbrennerian framework guided analyses. We coded interview data from family members and focal resident/paid caregiver interviews concerning the information provided about displacement over time (e.g., worries and concerns about the transition, including special therapies and caregiver sensitivities), with special attention to insights into the health and well-being of the focal resident.

Level	Examples of Guiding Categories
Individual – Focal Resident of TC	Length of time in TC, age, disability status and functional abilities; medical fragility
Family	Parent, sibling, family role and involvement as related to individual (aging, geographical distance, expertise)
Strategies for negotiating with systems	Role of care provider, specific care plans, variety of services received, advocacy
Community impacts (stakeholders, TC caregivers and administrators)	Availability of suitable group homes, volunteers such as faith leaders, business leaders, role of educational institutions and social services.
Competing needs for resources (policy)	Transparency of resources, waivers, state vs. local funding, costs in geographic areas

Table 1. Guiding Categories.

Preliminary Data Analysis of the Transitions

Based on our preliminary data, we established the following broad categories for coding. In Table 2, each of the five categories is listed with a corresponding quote and preliminary analysis of each based on our qualitative analytic approach.

System Level & Concept	Participant Quote with Relevance to Transition	Provisional Analysis
Resident Medical Fragility	He had pneumonia twice this winter. She has the mind of a two year old.	Parent wonders and worries about how a group home with part-time wage caregivers who can change can be mindful of subtle signs of bronchitis and pneumonia.
Family Role	I don't find it a burden to make these decisions. He is my brother.	It's part of being the brother to be responsible for decisions about group home setting.
Family Role & Chronosystem	I'm 70 years old. How will I be able to visit him?	As parent ages, the geographic distance of different group home options could be a barrier to visiting.
Strategies for Negotiating Systems & Policies	We were concerned that we would be discriminated against because we were so active in the resistance to the closures.	Parent expresses awareness that they are known by the state system and might be targeted as intrusive, affecting child's placement in group home.
Community	They don't realize that we had a whole system of 100 volunteers that came to the Center to visit them.	Informant recognizes the level of social and community connection that was present at TC, wonders how residents of group homes will have social and community lives.

Table 2. Sample Analytic Level Approaches.

Below, we highlight participants' respondes to and coping strategies for Virginia's plans to close most of the TCs and relocate residents in community settings. In the process of narrating the intricacies involved in relocating from a TC, the interviewees revealed three main concepts with respect to the transition process: 1) the idiosyncratic nature of medical fragility that hampers community placement, 2) stress caused by uncertainties surrounding the transition process, and 3) the crucial role of advocacy during and after the transition. Although these categories are not mutually exclusive or fully representative of the richness of the data, these three elements allow us to explore important intersections across these interviews that reveal how the process of moving institutionalized individuals into community settings is affects both family members and legal guardians.

1.) Idiosyncratic nature of medical fragility hampering community placement

The most prominent theme expressed in the interviews is how the idiosyncratic nature of medical fragility hampers community placement. For instance, when describing the care her son, David, needs, Nancy remarked, "He can't survive in my environment. He needs an environment tailored for him." Nancy is referring to her own home as her environment, which poses health risks for David, who needs 24-hour care, because his several medical complications could dangerously intersect with a home environment that has not been carefully curated. Nancy's husband, John, notes that if David is in a group home, generally innocuous objects his roommates might leave near him could pose potentially lethal choking hazards for David. This observation is representative of the kinds of details that slow down TC resident relocation; a number of community support systems must be in place before TC residents can be successfully and safely placed in the community.

Many families worry about their loved ones being moved to other intermediate care facilities that are farther away, leaving them unable to visit as often as in the past. A story reported in *The Hopewell News* profiles Susan and Howard Spielberg's son Jonathan, age 43, who has lived at SVTC for 20 years (Wilson, 2012). In addition to the Spielbergs' concerns about the for-profit nature of group homes, the couple is worried that the state and Department of Justice failed to consider that some individuals are best treated at the TCs. According to Mrs. Spielberg,

> We have believed, for 30 or more years, that the whole
> de-institutionalization movement is taking place based on
> a philosophical agenda that academicians primarily have,

that everybody can be served in the community, and we simply have not seen that that's a possibility.

Interviewees also note that because of the complexity of each resident's health needs, finding placements in the community that meet structural and staff needs has been more difficult than anticipated. In describing this difficulty, another interviewee, Anne, expressed satisfaction with the State of Virginia, who hired an out-of-state agency for consultation when placing her brother, who initially had no success being placed in communities that are a reasonable driving distance from his family members. It is worth mentioning here that this difficult community placement is not a universal experience, but because a majority of our interviewees are at the tail end of the relocation process, their family members and dependents are among the most medically fragile TC residents.

2) Stress and Uncertainty Surrounding the Transition Process

A second theme borne out in the interviews is how much stress the interviewees are under as they try to cope with uncertainty during the transition process. Several interviewees feared the instability of group homes and questioned whether their loved one's placement in a group home would be temporary or permanent. In addition to unknown details about future living arrangements, several family members disclosed that they had received conflicting information from various officials about the setup of group homes. For instance, Cindy, whose son has unpredictable mood swings, is afraid that her son might be evicted from a group home because of behavioral issues. Cindy remarked that she and her husband "just keep holding on" during the transition process and are focusing on advocating for their son so that he receives a community placement that meets his needs and is located within a reasonable driving distance of their home.

3) Crucial Role of Advocacy during and After Transition

Interviewees also focused on the importance of advocacy during and after the transition process. Both family members and public and private guardians voiced concerns about the state's ability to successfully place residents in community settings. At the heart of their concern was a perceived lack of coordination on the part of state and institution administration. For example, Nancy notes that surrogate decision makers are "very much left up to [their] own devices to piece together the support [they] need." Nancy uses support in two different contexts; she refers to both the support her son, David, needs, and the support that she and the rest of David's family needs during and after the transition process. She says that "the state has certified group homes as comparable when they are not comparable." Nancy turns the language of the state against itself, contradicting the word choice as well as the very idea of equivalence. Her statement is direct and spoken with authority; she is someone comfortable using legalistic language—"the state has certified"—but also feels knowledgeable and qualified to make that determination. Nancy functions not only as a casual advocate, but also speaks like a legal advocate because of her vast knowledge of the system. However, despite her vast knowledge and experience (as a parent volunteer at the Center for over 20 years), Nancy remains "cautious" when she expresses her concerns to her son's group home administrator. She is careful not to "sabotage" his care.

In other interviews conducted post-transition to group homes, family members noted confusion between administrative officials and staff members at group homes. Nancy remarked that the administrative official who had previously been a source of information about the transition has switched jobs, and she missed that source of support and individualized attention.

Like Nancy, Cindy observed that "the group home has so many changes in staff that I don't know who all these people are. I mean, I have a list, but I'm not good at memorizing and putting faces and people, and they change regularly. And when I ask a question [...] they don't know the answer, you know?" The list, meant to be a guide for this new place and system, is insufficient and places a difficult burden on the patient advocates to navigate staff changes. Language around uncertainty is pervasive: the interviewee is unfamiliar with the current staff, and the staff "don't know the answer" to many questions.

Though all the interviewees who criticize this lack of clear communication between stakeholders attribute it to nature of being in a transitory period, they also observe that, as one family member articulated, "if you don't have an active advocate, you're a forgotten soul when you're in the community." In this particular interview, though not stated explicitly, there is an obvious awareness that the resident's parents are aging and will be unable to advocate for their son much longer. Because there is an uncertainty about who will fill that advocacy role, the father worries his son will be "forgotten," not just as a physical body housed in a certain facility, but as a "soul." The connotation is that his son's fundamental personhood will be lost when his parents are no longer able to make people recognize him.

During this period of transition, other family member advocates have highlighted benefits of the *Olmstead* decision and Virginia's subsequent decision to move institutionalized individuals into community settings. One family wanted their son in the community much earlier but that said state officials encouraged them to move their son to a TC and used the TC "as an excuse not to provide community services." Later in the interview, the mother insisted that the state was "using this time [of transition] as a big gift" to advocate for more community services that are integral to their son's safety and happiness.

Discussion

We suspect that these early findings are illustrative of larger displacement issues. Our early data analysis demonstrates that surrogate decision makers for individuals with ID/DD in the process of being integrated into the community need highly individualized support from administrative officials during this transitory period. While a component of these interviews is how the idiosyncratic nature of ID/DD can hinder safe community placement, connections between these issues and the roles surrogate decision makers are embracing as advocates can serve as a heuristic for similar legal decisions being made in other states. Government and administrative officials charged with ensuring the safe placement of individuals in the most appropriate settings possible can use the data in this study to more effectively address stakeholders' concerns. While it may seem apparent that moving individuals with ID/DD from institutions into communities is a humane, rights-promoting, and resident-centered policy, Nancy's unanswered question, "how is it you feel [my son] is less restricted in a group home than he is in the center?" demonstrates the real and unresolved tension between communication between state officials making policy and family members directly involved with the implementation of that policy through the transition process.

Using participants' narrative rhetoric to describe a trajectory model of displacement enables linking the experience of displacement of individual residents with the perspectives of the family member(s), paid caregivers, and community stakeholders who are key actors in the process of displacement. Analysis of the participants' perceptions provides insights into ways the actors negotiate a trajectory of displacement involving the transition and care of the resident as well as the actors supporting the transition and its aftermath, all of which is intended to maximize the health and well-being of each resident, no matter their particular care requirements (Powell et al, 2015; Powell, 2013; Powell, 2015).

Next Steps for Studying the Transition

In order to develop a model of a trajectory of displacement, our next step is to employ a *phased process approach* for data collection, one in which the focal residents, their families, paid caregivers, and community stakeholders are interviewed throughout the trajectory of displacement. We believe that this approach will increase knowledge about vulnerable and medically fragile individuals and contribute to knowledge about displacement on a broader scale. An examination of participants' trajectories of displacement (i.e., prior to, during and post transition) allows the melding of perspectives vis a vis both rhetorical and narrative analysis (Andrews, 2014; Andrews et. al., 2001) supported by a qualitative grounded theory approach that focuses on underlying identities that are evoked and shaped by the process of transition (Charmez, 2006). Its systemic, socioecological, and longitudinal focus, invites deep insights about the complexity of factors that combine across time and location to shape trajectories of health and well-being throughout the experience of being displaced.

Conclusion

Across more than 100 years of history, the treatment of individuals with ID/DD has evolved from outright abuse, neglect, and utter abrogation of rights to the recognition, most recently and powerfully through *Olmstead,* that such individuals should live in the least restrictive environment possible. Litigation and resultant policies concerning expanding the rights of individuals with ID/DD have resulted in the transition of moving adults from a campus-based total institution to those more integrated into community settings such as group homes. While some advocates regard this movement as an important and positive step forward, our preliminary data suggest that other residents, family, and staff reveal a different story. Rather than regarding the TCs as locations of embarrassment and disempowerment, they seem them as locations fostering community and empowerment. For many, the TCs are repositories of services and care that may be difficult or impossible to replicate elsewhere. The real concerns of the surrogate decision makers for the residents speak to care requirements of residents who are medically fragile with unique needs. The decision makers are encountering mixed messages regarding the placement of their loved one, and understandably, are stressed because of the uncertainties of the present and future environment.

Currently, three of the five TCs remain open, with closures of two anticipated in 2018 and 2020. Of the Centers that have been shuttered, hundreds of residents have been moved to group homes while other residents are in stasis until appropriate housing can be secured. It is not surprising that the surrogate decision makers for the residents insist that they must remain ever vigilant in their advocacy efforts, just as they have in past years. However, in the wake of the transition, it is difficult for them to discern the direction and focus of the advocacy of the future, as placement and service decisions are ongoing, evolving, and made without them. Rather than relevant actors in the life of their loved one, they fear that their loved one will become lost in an effort by the State that is compelling from a population rights perspective but dangerous at the level of the individual and his or her family. It may well be that the State, in its promotion of rights for a population of individuals heretofore without them has made a decision based on an academic, "philosophical agenda" reflecting a "one-size-fits-all" conception of institutionalization. While laudable on many levels, its implementation may make a highly vulnerable population even more vulnerable to state abuses by failing to consider very real and detrimental effects this state-imposed transition will have on some of Virginia's most vulnerable (and unique) citizens—before, during, and after the transition and for years to come.

References

Allen, K.G. (2001). Long-Term Care: Implications of Supreme Court's Olmstead Decision are Still Unfolding. *GAO Testimony before the Special Committee on Aging*; U.S. Senate.

Americans with Disabilities Act of 1990, Pub. L. No. 101-336, Stat. 327.

Andrews, M. (2014). *Narrative Imagination and Everyday Life*. Oxford: Oxford University Press.

Andrews, M., Sclater S.D., Rustin M., Squire C., & Treacher A. (2001). Introduction. *Lines of Narrative: Psychosocial Perspectives*. M. Andrews, S.D. Sclater, C. Squire, A. Treacher, N.K. Denzin (Eds.). New York: Routledge.

Baines, E.K. (2004). *Vulnerable Bodies: Gender, the UN and the Global Refugee Crisis*. Burlington, VT: Ashgate Publishing.

Barber, J.G., Cooper, B.K., & Owen L. (1994). The Short-Term Effects of Relocation on the Intellectually Disabled. *Research on Social Work Practice*, 4(2), 248-258.

Bekhet, A.K., & Zauszniewski, J.A. (2014). Psychometiric Preterits of the Index of Relocation Adjustment. *Journal of Applied Gerontology*, 33(4), 437-455.

Benjamin v. Department of Public Welfare, 1:09-cv-1182 (2009).

Bronfenbrenner, U. (1979). *The Ecology of Human Development: Experiments by Nature and Design*. Cambridge, MA: Harvard University Press.

Caley, S.B., & Caley, S.D. (2010). The Olmstead Decision: The Road to Dignity and Freedom. *Georgia State University Law Review*, 26(3), 651-662.

Charmaz, K. (2006). *Constructing grounded theory: A practical guide through qualitative analysis.* Thousand Oaks, CA: Sage.

Cooper, B., & Picton, C. (2000). The Long-term effects of relocation on people with an intellectual disability: Quality of life, behavior, and environment. *Research on Social Work Practice,* 10(2), 195-208.

Currell, S., & Cogdell, C. (Eds.). (2006). *Popular Eugenics: National Efficiency and American Mass Culture in the 1930s.* Athens: Ohio University Press.

Daily Press Health Report (2015 March 14). *Medicaid waiver wait lists growing for Virginians.* Retrieved from http://www.dailypress.com/health/dp-fea-health-notes-0314-20150314-story.html

Dodson, L., & Schmalzbauer, L. (2005). Poor Mothers and Habits of Hiding: Participatory Methods in Poverty Research. *Journal of Marriage & Family,* 67(4), 949-959.

Dorr, G.M. (2008). *Segregation's Science: Eugenics and Society in Virginia.* Charlottesville, VA: University of Virginia Press.

Fletcher, D. J. (2013 December 3). *Third Report of the Independent Reviewer.* Retrieved from https://www.justice.gov/sites/default/files/crt/legacy/2013/12/13/va-ada_thirdrevrrpt_12-6-13.pdf

Gilgun, J. F. (2005). Qualitative research and family psychology. *Journal of Family Psychology, 19*(1), 40-50.

Glaser, B., & Strauss, A. (1967). *The discovery of grounded theory: Strategies for qualitative research.* Chicago, IL: Aldine Publishing Company.

Goffman, E. (1968). Asylums: Essays on the social situation of mental patients and other inmates. Aldine Transaction.

Hsieh, H., & Shannon, S. E. (2005). Three approaches to qualitative content analysis. *Qualitative Health Research, 15,* 1277-1288. doi:10.1177/1049732305276687

Kleiner, S. (2016 September 1) Redesign of Virginia's waiver program for people with disabilities takes effect. *Richmond Times-Dispatch.* Retrieved from http://www.richmond.com/article_4f924e49-c6f5-5768-a977-0b9fcc7b07e2.html

Knapp, S.J. (2002). Authorizing Family Science: An Analysis of the Objectifying Practices of Family Science Discourse. *Journal of Marriage & Family,* 64(4), 1038-1048.

Kozma, A., Mansell, J., & Beadle-Brown, J. (2009). Outcomes in different residential settings for people with intellectual disability: A systematic review. *American Association on Intellectual and Developmental Disabilities*, 114(3), 193–222.

Lakin, K.C., Prouty, R., Polister, B., & Coucouvants, K. (2003). Change in residential placements for persons with intellectual and developmental disabilities in the USA in the last two decades. *Journal of Intellectual & Developmental Disability*, 28(2), 205–210.

Lareau, A. (2012). Using the terms hypothesis and variable for qualitative work: A critical reflection. *Journal of Marriage and Family*, 74, 671–677.

Larson, S.A., Salmi, P., Smith, D., Anderson, L., & Hewitt, A.S. (2013). Residential services for persons with intellectual or developmental disabilities: Status and trends through 2011. Minneapolis, MN: University of Minnesota, Research and Training Center on Community Living, Institute on Community Integration.

Lombardo, P. (2008). *Three Generations, No Imbeciles: Eugenics, the Supreme Court, and Buck v. Bell.* Baltimore: Johns Hopkins University Press.

Lord, J., & Hearn, C. (1987). *Return to the Community: The process of closing an institution.* Ontario: Centre for Research and Education in Human Services.

National Council on Disability (2014) NCD Statement on the 15th Anniversary of the Olmstead Decision. Retrieved from http://www.ncd.gov/NCD/newsroom/06232014

Nielson, K. (2012). *A Disability History of the United States.* Boston: Beacon Press.

Olmstead v. L.C., 527 U.S. at 587 (1999).

Olmstead, Commissioner, Georgia Department of Human Resources, et al. v. L.C., 527 U.S. 581 (1999).

Patti, P.J., Amble, K.B., & Flory, M.J. (2005). Life events in older adults with intellectual disabilities: Differences between adults with and without Down syndrome. *Journal of Policy and Practice in Intellectual Disabilities*, 2(2),149–155.

Patti, P., Amble, K., & Flory, M. (2010). Placement, relocation and end of life issues in aging adults with and without Down's syndrome: A retrospective study. *Journal of Intellectual Disability Research*, 54(6), 538–546.

Perez, T. E. (2011 February 10). *Central Virginia Training Center Findings Letter*. Retrieved from https://www.justice.gov/sites/default/files/crt/legacy/2011/03/01/cvtc_findlet_02-10-2011.pdf

Potter, D. (2012, January 27). Virginia must close four of five of its 'training centers' for the disabled. *Daily Press*. Retrieved from http://www.dailypress.com/health/dp-nws-training-centers-for-the-disbled-20120127-story.html

Powell, K.M, Dick-Mosher, J., Zvonkovic, A., & Teaster, P. (2015). Displacing Marginalized Bodies: How Human Rights Discourses Function in the Law and in Communities. *Journal of Semiotics of the Law*, 29(1), 67-85.

Powell, K.M. (2015). *Identity and Power in Narratives of Displacement*. New York: Routledge.

Powell, K.M. (2013). Converging Crises: Rhetorical Constructions of Eugenics and the Public Child. *JAC: Journal of Rhetoric, Culture, and Politics* 33(3): 455-486.

Sciarrillo, Rosemary v. Christopher Christie and the State of New Jersey. CIV. NO.: 2:13-cv-03478. Retrieved from http://www.ada.gov/olmstead/documents/sciarrillo-christie-soi.pdf.

The ADA and Olmstead Enforcement: Ensuring Community Opportunities for Individuals with Disabilities. (2013). S. Hrg. 111-696 Washington, DC: Government Printing Office.

Southwest Virginia Training Center (2016, June 28). *Services*. Retrieved from http://www.swvtc.dbhds.virginia.gov/services.htm.

Rosenbaum, S. & Teitelbaum, J. (2004). Olmstead at five: Assessing the impact. Washington, DC: U.S. Government Printing Office.

Steel, Z., Chey, T. Silove, D., Marnane, C., Bryant, R.A. vanOmmeren, M. (2009). Association of Torture and Other Potentially Traumatic Events with Mental Health Outcomes Among Populations Exposed to Mass Conflict and Displacement. *Journal of the American Medical Association*, 302(5), 537-549.

Stefan, S. (2010). Beyond Residential Segregation: The Application of the Olmstead Decision to Segregated Employment Settings. *Georgia*

State University Law Review, 26(3), 875-919.

Stewart III, J.W. (2013 February 11). Update on the closure of Southside Virginia Training Center. Retrieved from http://hac.state.va.us/subcommittee/Training_Centers_Closure_Joint_Sub/02-11-13/2013%2002%2011%20-%20Joint%20Special%20Subcommittee%20DBHDS.pdf

Swenson, A., Zvonkovic, A. M., Rojas-McWhinney, J., & Gerst, K. (2015). A couple analysis of relationship perception among couples who face work demands. *Personal Relationships, 22*, 153–171.

Trent, J.W. (2006). Intellectual Disabilities in the USA: From the Institution to the Community, 1948–2001. In John Welshman and Jan Walmsley (Eds.), *Community Care in Perspective: Care, Control and Citizenship*. New York: Palgrave Macmillan. 109–121.

Trent, J.W. (1994). *Inventing the Feeble Mind: A History of Mental Retardation in the United States*. Berkeley: University of California Press.

United Nations (2013). Convention on the rights of persons with disabilities. Retrieved from http://www.un.org/disabilities/default.asp?navid=14&pid=150.

United States of America v. Commonwealth of Virginia and Peggy Wood, et al., 3:12CV59-JAG (2012).

Virginia Department of Behavioral Health and Developmental Services. (2013). *My New Home in the Community: An Information Handbook for Families Preparing to Transition from Institutions to New Homes in the Community*. Retrieved from http://www.dbhds.virginia.gov/documents/ODS/My%20New%2Home%20in%20the%0Community.pdf

Welshman, J., & Walmsley, J. (Eds.). (2006). *Community Care in Perspective: Care, Control and Citizenship*. New York: Palgrave Macmillan.

Wilson, S. (2012 April 26). Families speak on DOJ's and Commonwealth's settlement. *The Hopewell Settlement*. Retrieved from http://www.hopewellnews.com/news/exec/view.pl?archive=3&num=4451#.WA90HpMrL-Z

Woodman, A.C., Mailick, M.R., Anderson, K.A., & Esbensen, A.J. (2014). Residential Transitions among Adults with Intellectual Disability across 20 years. *American Journal of Developmental Disability*, 119(6),

496-515.

Young, L., Sigafoos, J., Suttie, J., Ashman, A., Grevell, P. (1998). Deinstitu-
    tionalisation of persons with intellectual disabilities: A review of
    Australian studies. *Journal of Intellectual and Developmental Disabil-
    ity*, 23(2), 155-170.

Zendell, A. L. (2007). Impact of the olmstead decision five years later: A
    national perspective for social workers. *Journal of Gerontological
    Social Work,*49(1/2), 97-113.

Zvonkovic, A., Powell, K., Smith, C. J. (2014). Displacement over time: A
    life course perspective on globalization for workers and families.
    In Christine A. Readdick (Ed.), *Irish families and globalization: con-
    versations about belonging and identity across space and time* (pp.161-
    180). *Groves Monographs on Marriage and Family (vol. 3)*. Ann Arbor:
    University of Michigan.

Chapter Three

Impression management: How people with aphasia and their caregiver partners navigate front and back stage

Tessa le Roux

Lasell College

On The Stage

They were actors and actresses; they were all dancers,
Always swaying to the melodies,
Their arms and pointed palms leaping above.
What would they be like from the balcony?

The orchestra was on the ground floor.
Tapping their feet, step by step,
There was an overwhelming applause,
An audience, no one had paused to see.

Altogether, they were theatre lovers, and
They were there too!
How many "Curtain Calls" will be?
Overtime, to imagine that view!

From: Aphasia, and Eureka! By Leonard Zion

Aphasia is a language disorder caused by stroke, head injury, and disease. When a person's ability to communicate effectively is impaired, the ways in which they perform their social roles are affected. An acquired disability presents people with new roles which they had little or no rehearsal for. In the case of stroke and aphasia, their problems are compounded by the fact that their language is affected.

In family studies analysis of interaction in terms of roles, within a symbolic interactionist framework, is commonly used. Through the process of socialization we internalize the expectations of roles, such as husband, wife, mother, or child. This is a very useful approach in a study of mental health, disability and the caregiver role, especially as it pertains to stress, role conflict, role overload and so forth. Aphasia clearly affects the ability to interact and perform social roles.

Goffman's work, however, goes beyond the typical symbolic interactionist view of role. In Presentation of Self in Everyday Life (1959) Goffman used the metaphor of a stage or drama to explain how identity is presented. The metaphor of a stage performance provides a useful set of conceptual tools to analyse role performance in a more nuanced way. It provides an avenue for acknowledging people's agency – they are actively busy performing for an audience, hence interpreting roles so as to control the impression they make.

In recent years Goffman's classical work on presentation of self has seen a revival, especially in studies of presentation of self in the online world (e.g. Hogan, 2010, and Bullingham & Vasconcelos, 2013). Though the concept of presentation of self is widely used, his work contains many other concepts that have merit. In this paper I illustrate how Goffman's theory can be used as a conceptual framework for understanding the experiences of people living with aphasia, as well as their caregivers. In true Goffman tradition, I will draw on a variety of sources to describe the "presentation of self in everyday life" of aphasics and their caregiver spouses/partners. I base my discussion on a variety of sources, including academic literature as well as memoirs, films, materials produced by support and advocacy groups, and my observations during my own participation in various aphasia support groups, rehabilitative services, and conferences.

Aphasia

Aphasia is a neurological disorder which brings about difficulty in expressing oneself when speaking, trouble understanding speech, and difficulty with reading and writing. The most common cause of aphasia is stroke – about 25 to 40 percent of stroke survivors have aphasia (National Aphasia Association, 2018). Stroke, in turn, is commonly regarded as one of the leading causes of serious, long-term adult disability – for example, in the US approximately 800,000 people suffer a stroke every year (National Stroke Association, 2018).

While many aphasics are stroke survivors (about 90% of aphasics have suffered a stroke), this language disorder can also be caused by traumatic brain injury, infections or inflammations, brain tumours or degenerative conditions including dementia. It is estimated that about 1 in 250 people in the US have aphasia (Ganzfield, 2016, p. 1). Although the majority of aphasics are older, the incidence of young aphasia is increasing due to improved survival rates after war, car accidents, and drug overdose.

The severity of aphasia is determined by the location and size of the damaged area in the brain. In some cases there is rapid spontaneous improvement, in other cases some degree of improvement can continue for a long period. Aphasia can take many forms. Commonly multiple aspects of communication are impaired – talking, comprehension, reading and writing. It can, however, affect mainly a single aspect of language use such as the ability to retrieve the names of objects, or the ability to put words together into sentences. In some cases aphasics can produce few recognizable words and understand little or no spoken language, in other cases they are limited to short utterances of less than four words. They may simply have a limited vocabulary, or may have the inability to produce certain categories of words such as verbs or nouns. They may have fluent speech with no content or have output full of vague circumlocutions and expressions of frustration. In other words aphasia can present in many different ways, but ultimately, language and hence communication, is affected (Krishner, 1995, Menifee, 2000). Furthermore, as Greenfield (2016) points out, "Aphasia affects speech and language, but the whole person ultimately is affected by the experience. The psychological and social self struggles to understand a changed path and significant revision of life goals and dreams" (p.10). Or, as Lauren Marks, in her memoir (2017) so eloquently puts it, ""The Girl I Used to Be had built up a life for twenty-seven years. The Woman I was Becoming had only eight months under her belt. And these two lives existed in patches and scraps, divided in separate heaps…" (p. 242).

A common care model utilized by speech and language therapists is the so-called Person- and family-centred care, which is "a collaborative approach grounded in a mutually beneficial partnership among individuals, families, and clinicians. Each party is equally important in the relationship, and each party respects the knowledge, skills, and experiences that the others bring to the process" (American Speech-Language-Hearing Association). Caregivers are therefore not only involved in activities of daily living, household activities, financial planning and social engagement. They are often also actively involved in the rehabilitative process. The focus in this paper is on those with aphasia who have caregiver spouses or partners. We turn, therefore, very briefly to the nature of caregiving in contemporary US society.

Caregiving

The de-institutionalization movement has brought about a shift in the way disability is perceived in our society and there is strong emphasis on independence. The shift towards inclusion of families in rehabilitation, therapy and care of the disabled also coincides with a move in medical care towards a more inclusive model. More patients are asking to be seen as partners, and a more holistic model of health care is increasingly being demanded. Language, occupational and physical therapy is geared toward "community re-entry" and "activities of daily living" – even cognitive therapy is moving away from clinical settings towards a model based on home environment.

We should also not lose sight of the fact that upwards of 75% of family caregivers in the US are female (Family Caregiver Alliance, 2016); they are wives, mothers, sisters, and daughters, and most of them are older women. Because of the persistence of traditional gender roles women are the ones who identify with the caregiver role. Providing care at home is treated as a taken-for-granted, unpaid role, which is taken on willingly and without question. The perceived privacy of family issues reinforces this notion.

Crimmons (2000) tells the story of her husband's rehabilitation after head injury – in a particularly desperate moment, someone reminds her that she married him "for better or for worse", and that she is now dealing with the "worse" part of that deal. The complexity of a loving care giving relationship, coupled with societal expectations, inhibit any critique of a system in which care is relegated to family members, mostly women. Thus the goal is to appear as "normal" as possible – for many this means presenting the face of a happy marriage/relationship, with an independent, decision-making male and a supportive wife/partner. Public and private are kept separate and the face that is presented to the world is one of dignity and unity.

The Dramaturgical Approach of Goffman

In her memoir, Carol Maloney (2013) describes what it is like to lack the words to share your thoughts through the metaphor of being the keynote speaker at a national convention – the PowerPoint is good, and the presenter is well-prepared. She continues, "You walk to the podium, look out at the audience, and suddenly you are unable to say a word. Your throat is in a spasm, you become more and more nervous, all the facts are jumbled in your mind, and you cannot say a word. This is similar to what people with aphasia live every day" (p.46).

Goffman similarly used the metaphor of the stage for all human interaction. He distinguished between the *front region* (or *front stage*) where people *perform* in front of an audience and the *back region*. It is backstage that individuals prepare for their roles. When performing in *front* people act out their roles in order to make the best *impression*. This includes both their manner and their *appearance* – which includes the dress and look of the performer. But Goffman goes further than just the metaphor of interaction between a person and an audience. He incorporates more elements of a stage performance. His model also looks at the way performers might work together in *teams* and form *bonds* of collegiality based on their common commitment to a performance they are both engaged in. In addition, the stage includes *props*, and there is an *audience*. And because interaction is a two-way process, the actor is also an audience for another actor or set of actors.

In much of life roles are pre-established, the front, costume and props are well-known and clearly established for each specific audience. The actor mainly has to keep to the script and adapt as needed. Thus the individual conforms but also has agency. Everyone involved in a social situation works together to support the actor in performing the role according to script – and if something goes wrong, causing an embarrassing moment, there are attempts to help create a sense of normalcy so that actors can *save face*.

Clearly in the case of aphasia, where communication is hindered, there is a disruption of the typical performance and managing impression is much harder. In the rest of this paper, I will use Goffman's conceptual scheme to illustrate this process with examples from the various memoirs and observations.

Giving expression

> "I my…family… they'll lose you essence, so I try very
> hard to forget it you know, what to say. Or I just sit in one
> side. Just try to ignoring."…."All a sudden, the gone. Bye
> bye."…(the voice of Ravi, an aphasic man in Parr, Byng
> and Gilpin, 1997, p. 52).

The words above express a common experience. A language disorder does not only lead to a loss of familiar employment, with consequent social isolation, but also the disruption of family roles and the depression associated with the frustrations of being disabled. The person with a language disorder is also at a disadvantage in terms of giving expression (in Goffman's conceptual scheme) – using symbols to convey information. We present ourselves in ways to create a certain impression, and to influence the definition of a situation. Kimberley Williams-Paisley (2017) whose mother developed primary progressive aphasia at a young age describes how her mother avoided recognizing the problem, "Her… intentions came from a good place. She didn't want anyone to be worried. She didn't want them to be embarrassed or feel exposed."

The importance of language in social interaction is underlined by the experiences of those who have lost language. In the foreword to Helen Wulf's memoir, "Aphasia, my world alone", speech pathologist Rolnick states, "Man's ability to communicate must certainly be the outstanding factor that sets him apart from the rest of the animal kingdom. Sudden and unexpected loss of communication is a terrifying, dehumanizing experience that tears away at the essence of life itself" (In Wulf, 1997, p.9).

In her poignant memoir in which Sheila Hale describes life with her highly educated historian husband John after his stroke, she writes, "If the story of aphasia has had no such happy ending, the reason is that most of us can't help judging the quality of thought – of our own thinking as well as that of others – by the language in which it is expressed. By what other means can you know what another person is thinking? How, without language, can you know what you yourself are thinking?" (Hale 2007, p.196).

It is precisely because of this "judging the quality of thought" that Hale refers to above, that aphasics have an additional barrier to overcome – people assume they lack understanding (cognitive ability). While some forms of aphasia do impact comprehension, many aphasics are simply unable to express their thoughts. Despite the National Aphasia Association's attempts to emphasize that loss of language does not mean loss of intelligence, the inability to communicate clearly interferes with the ability to, in Goffman's words, give expression to presentation of self. In her memoir Carol Schultz (2010) writes, "It is unfortunate in our society that intelligence is too often equated with one's speech dexterity. Because I speak so poorly, some assume I do not have thoughts in my head. Therefore, they think I do not have intelligence. I know I have thoughts, but without words to express them, my intelligence is suspect" (p. 107).

For people with disabilities or special needs language is particularly important, not only in giving expression, but also "in maintaining relationships, in negotiating and controlling the help that is given, and in understanding and coping with a suddenly acquired, long-term impairment." (Parr, Byng and Gilpin, 1997, p.xii). Nina Mitchell, a young Harvard graduate describes her feelings of helplessness at the loss of identity after a stroke:

> I was not angry, just profoundly resigned….I simply shook my head….I just surrendered to the force that wanted me to be silent….Some liken aphasia to being dropped in a foreign country where no one speaks your language. But in that scenario, you would at least be confident that you had speech – a comfort, even if you couldn't find a bathroom. But to open my mouth with some idea of what I wanted to say and have nothing, nothing came out, was true frustration. Language is what makes us human, what

separates us from the animals. Aphasia makes you feel like
a beast, no matter how eloquent you are inside.

Thus stroke and head injury bring about a traumatic and sudden
change in self. In her memoir, Wulf writes about her own experiences
and realization of her impairment. She says "every aphasic must learn the
feeling of being imprisoned within himself" (1997, p.13). She describes the
following situation:

> At this moment, when my various selves were in different
> realities at once, two of the hospital personnel came into
> my room. 'Well', I thought, 'wouldn't it be nice to tell
> somebody about a marvellous feeling. Why not these
> two?' Forgotten was the painful fact that I could not
> talk properly. With considerable internal enthusiasm I
> plunged into a description of an experience without peer.
> Too late the truth flooded through me! *My speech was
> almost unintelligible! I could not communicate!*

> But what a disaster! The fury I felt at myself, and no way
> to explain it, was great enough to cause brief tears. My
> fate thereby was sealed. My automatic defences decided
> that I should never again mention to anyone in the
> hospital what was to me an experience of melding into
> a zenith of comprehension and wonder....The moment
> when I was eager to share an experience became very
> nearly the same moment when the realization of my
> inability to communicate normally literally bombed
> me. It must have been then that my self-respect was
> delivered a tottering blow "(1979:35). One is reminded of
> Goffman's description, in a later work, Stigma (1963), of
> seeing oneself as disabled in the mirror and not seeing it –
> expecting the "real" self and then the shock.

She describes trying to communicate as follows: "Aphasia finds the
mind struggling as it seeks ways to push a thought, one thought, any
thought through a banged up brain to the world outside where it can be
interpreted by other mortals not damaged by aphasia. Do these outsiders
have the qualities of imagination and perception? Think of the ways there
are to communicate: speaking, signals, symbols, sounds, expressions,
pantomime, drawing, writing – innumerable ways. The aphasic
communicates in ways he hopes will be meaningful to those around him.
The difficulty lies with his interpreters." (1979, p.142)
Wulf's frustration relates to the fact that she is unable to utilize

the normal ritual and cooperation involved in face-work. According to
Goffman the social value we claim for ourselves in interpersonal contact
depends on a line, or pattern of verbal and nonverbal acts by which
we express ourselves. (Goffman, 1959, pp. 213-231). In the case of the
aphasic, the situation is complicated by the fact that many people with
aphasia have no visibly detectable disability. An aphasic, Alf, says,
"You can see a person in a wheelchair...he or she got no legs. Then
you say, 'Oh yes. That person is disabled.' But you cannot see that I am
aphasic. They cannot see it, so how will they know? Have I got a notice
board up and you say: 'I am aphasic?" (In Parr, Byng and Gilpin, 1997,
p.118). Thus people with aphasia often have a hidden disability. Or
in Goffman's language – the set is misleading because the audience
expects someone with "normal" communication ability and are caught
off-guard. The person with aphasia's ability to manage impression with
strangers is hampered, and as Goffman points out, there is a *continuum
in misrepresentation* – in other words if the actor is discredited in one
area this throws doubt on the others. For example, because someone is
unable to produce fluent language, an aphasic who actually has intact
comprehension may be treated as if he or she had diminished cognitive
ability. Likewise many people tend to raise their voices when talking to
someone with aphasia, assuming that the person is also hard of hearing.
Maloney (2013) says, "People's reactions to my aphasia and hand
movements are varied. Their body language tells me that people are
puzzled as to why I am doing this. Some people look away as I talk or
ignore me. Others just lower their eyes and listen" (p.52).

   Impression management with friends or family, on the other
hand, may take a different course than with strangers. Communication
frequently relies on things other than language. For example, John Hale
communicates with intonation. He does not produce real words, instead
he repeats a single syllable "whoas, whoas" that sounds like speech. His
wife writes,

> From then on we have continued to talk about whatever
> is on our minds, almost as we did before his stroke. Often
> is is just chat about the feel of the moment we are sharing:
> the taste of a glass of wine, the pain of a toothache, the
> fragrance and colours of plants in our garden. Sometimes
> I ask him what it feels like to have no words. And he
> answers me in his long, richly nuanced sentences, his
> voice rising, falling, emphasizing, pausing for thought,
> qualifying as naturally as though he were explaining
> to an eager student some particularly interesting but
> complicated moment in the history of the European

Renaissance. I don't always understand exactly what he is saying, but I think I may have a better idea of what it is like to be John just from the sound of his voice when he exclaims at the sight of our bright red azalea, always the first spells of vivid colour after the long, dreary English winter, and from the way he pretends to warm his hands in front of it on chilly spring days. (Hale 2007:60).

In Goffman's scheme, the actor is the one responsible for creating impression. In the case of the aphasic, who is not always able to convey a message, whether verbally or non-verbally, he or she is not always successful, and moreover, may not be aware of the lack of success. In fact the lines between actor and audience may become somewhat blurred. Hale writes:

Nevertheless Elizabeth [speech therapist] had very gently, without ever insisting, begun to persuade me that John's prosodic flow, however apparently in tune with a subject under discussion, did not actually represent real words or sentences. The fact that he thought they did was part of his problem. He wasn't 'monitoring' his output. Sometimes, when people confessed that they could not understand what he was saying, he would react by slowing down, speaking more emphatically as though to rephrase and clarify his point. But sometimes, when they guessed at his meaning, and he agreed with their verbalized interpretation, I suspected that he had done so mainly in order to please them and to keep them talking (2007:173).

Goffman's distinction between front and back is relevant here. The front region is like the stage front in a theatrical performance – actors both on the stage and in social life are interested in appearances. The front includes items of expressive equipment such as rank, clothing, sex, age, gestures, and facial expressions. These are all impacted in aphasics. The audience expects coherence of these, but this does not exist in case of an aphasic individual. The back region is where actors shed their roles and can be themselves (1959, p.362). When communication is compromised as in the case of aphasia, the boundaries between front and back can become blurred. Harrianne Mills, the aphasic writing about her own experiences quoted before concludes her book with these words: "The boundary between real and unreal, between self and the other, ceases to exist. Those kinds of distinctions are simply far too simplistic for the complex world in which an aphasic lives" (2004, p.25).

According to Goffman, failure to regulate the information acquired by the audience involves possible disruption of the projected definition of the situation (1959, p.67). Control over what is perceived is control over contact that is made between people. In the case of aphasia this control is deficient; in fact, he or she is to greater or lesser extent dependent on the audience to help define the situation. Hale, cited above, whose husband only utters modulated sounds, not words, laments the fact that she cannot " ask our friends to stop conspiring in the fiction that he makes sense when he talks" (p.178).

The advice from the National Aphasia Association about how to communicate with a person with aphasia provides an example of audience collaboration in assisting with communication, and by extension, of defining the situation. For example, "Minimize or eliminate background noise...Keep communication simple, but adult. Simplify your own sentence structure and reduce your rate of speech....Praise all attempts to speak and downplay any errors...Encourage independence and avoid being overprotective." (National Aphasia Association, n.d.). Likewise in a guide for speech-language pathologists, "Keep messages focused. One message at a time. Simplify long, complex directions, and break into verbal steps, if possible." (Holland, 1998, p.43).

In short, giving expression in the case of an aphasic is undermined by inability to communicate clearly and with intent, and limited by stereotypes. The boundary between front and back become blurred, and the aphasic is dependent on non-verbal communication and audience collaboration in the process of impression management.

Spouses and other significant others

The expectations that the marital relationship is private has implications for the willingness of spouses to seek help. Burack-Weiss did a content analysis of published memoirs of people caring for the disabled. She says, "Going public with a private matter marks a point of no return" (2006, p. 65). Furthermore, although the term caregiving normally refers to anyone who provides assistance to someone else who is incapacitated and needs help (Suthers, 2006, p.4), it is not without controversy. Within the disability rights movement "care" is regarded as colonization and control of disabled people – it locates power with the caregiver and assumes that the one cared for is passive and dependent. In order to decrease stigma and feelings of inadequacy in survivors of stroke and head injury, it has become common to refer to co-survivors rather than caregivers. This further reinforces the "united front". In other words it is not only the aphasic who manages impression.

While the aphasics have to manage impressions within the constraints of diminished language abilities, spouses or significant others also have to deal with a sudden change in roles. In their case the constraints are not the inability to communicate, but rather the societal expectations and a sense of loyalty or commitment to the person with aphasia.

Hale describes the realization that roles, and therefore the relationship, have changed in a fundamental way:

> "One evening in October all the friends happened to leave early. I was alone with John, facing him across the bedside locker on which I had laid out the supper that I'd cooked at home and warmed up in the hospital's microwave. ….I watched John preparing to enjoy his food and my company, and listened to his voice – da woahs, da woahs, da woahs? – asking me to talk to him tell him about my day. Suddenly I was tired, too tired to carry the burden of a one-sided conversation. I thought about all the married women I knew who said they preferred the company of their pet animals to having a man around: animals, they say, understand more than you think; they whine and purr and bark when you tell them your problems; some dogs even howl in tune to music. I was too weak to resist a quick, forbidden glance into the future. *And what I saw there was a succession of meals, sitting across a table from a husband who was no more, or less, companionable than an affectionate dog* (2007, p.59) (my emphasis).

It is not uncommon for memoirs written by the spouses of people who survive head injury or stroke to have similar descriptions of the realization that roles have changed. Yet this new definition of the situation is not shared with the recently disabled spouse. The relationship is not only altered because of the difficulties with communicating, and because one spouse takes on the role of caregiver or assistant communicator to the outside world, there is also the attempt to create a sense of normality, that the roles are still what they are, despite the new dependence of the aphasic on his or her spouse. There are probably many different reasons why spouses manage impression in this way: they want to protect their loved ones from the truth, they want to motivate and encourage them, and they have a hard time admitting the reality of the situation to themselves. In addition they may be *idealizing* – according to Goffman the notion that individuals tend, in their performance, to incorporate and exemplify the officially accredited values of the society (Goffman 1959, p.35).

In all relationships there is some impression management, including in marriage. Goffman (1959) describes how people hide what they really feel about the other and - the maintenance of a surface of agreement, a veneer of consensus facilitated by each participant "concealing their own wants behind statements which assert values to which everyone present feels obliged to give lip service"(p.9). And later, "In constructing the overall definition of a situation, individuals engage in performances in which each orchestrates gestures to 'present oneself' in a particular manner as a person having identifiable characteristics and deserving of treatment in a certain fashion" (1959, p.397). Disability (including aphasia) leads to a special case of impression management. Montgomery-West (1995, p.2) describes how life under these circumstances takes on a quality of 'walking on egg-shells". In fact spouses work very hard at creating the impression that things are approximating "normality" – they attempt to make life appear as similar as possible to what it was "before". Many caregivers describe things they do to make their husband think that they are still in charge; they create opportunities for the disabled person to make choices. A wife describes during a support group meeting how she hides the fact that she hires someone to help manage the family finances from her husband, and allows him to think that he is making the decisions.

This idealization has to be seen in the context of the gendered nature of care giving. According to Goffman participants in an encounter together create a single over-all definition of the real situation "which involves not so much a real agreement as to what exists but rather a real agreement as to whose claims concerning what issues will be temporarily honored" (195, pp.9-10). It seems that, very frequently, within the marriage with an aphasic, there is no *collaborative* agreement on a definition of the situation, as suggested by Goffman above. Instead, spouses opt to create the impression of an agreement. The "pretence of normalcy" is maintained, at least by the non-aphasic partner. An example is the husband caregiver of S., a stroke survivor in her fifties. She attends one of the weekly aphasia groups I observed. S. is unable to produce any language. Her comprehension is fairly well preserved, however, and she suffers from severe depression because of her inability to express herself. Her husband tells other caregivers how he goes into the basement of their house when he finds things intolerable. He hits something, and yells at the top of his voice to release his frustrations and then goes back up to her with a smile on his face, saying, "Yes, my dear, what do you want?" In similar vein, a husband of an aphasic woman writes in a letter to the editor of Stroke (a journal of the National Stroke Association), about the pretence of joyfulness,"… in our home, the Pollyanna outlook that is stressed causes extreme frustration, anger and rage since it is our feeling that, … you understandably want to put a positive face on the problems stroke survivors face…".

While there is always some impression management in encounters, including in marriage, the married couple also create impression *as a unit.* Goffman's work on teams provides us with the conceptual framework to consider this. A team refers to a set of individuals who co-operate in staging a single routine (1959, p.79). In the sense that the aphasic individual is dependent on someone else (in this case their spouse) to help him or her communicate, this concept is particularly relevant. There is a dependency relationship which is not publicly admitted, so, whereas Goffman states that team members "…will hardly be in a position to maintain that particular impression before one another", it can be argued that in many aphasic relationships, this private admission is also absent.

In the case of the teams Goffman describes, team members cooperate to present a sense of normality to the world at large – the front region. At the same time there is the back region, where actors might admit their discomfort or frustration with their roles. In practice this means that a "normal" couple might put up a front when they are presenting themselves as a couple (or team, in Goffman's conceptual scheme). In private, however, the "curtain is down" and there is open communication, which can include conflict. In the case of a couple where one partner is disabled, and, in the case of aphasia, dependent on the other for much of his or her communication, this open admission of personal emotions and feelings is less common.

"In constructing the overall definition of a situation, individuals engage in performances in which each orchestrates gestures to 'present oneself' in a particular manner as a person having identifiable characteristics and deserving of treatment in a certain fashion" (Goffman, 1959, p.397). In the case of aphasics plus spouses this is somewhat of a joint effort – the aphasic-plus- spouse team presents a particular definition of the situation, which is in line with societal expectations. In fact, says Goffman, "…one often finds that someone is given the right to direct and control the progress of the dramatic action". Clearly this is the partner who is able to communicate. Yet the impression that is created is one of a unified front, and typically of a wife deferring to her husband.

In conclusion, then, it seems that the spouse-caregiver of the aphasic is almost exclusively acting in a front region – whether inside the marriage, or as part of a couple-team facing others. This inevitably leads to stress. In fact, a review of the literature tells us that caregivers can have significant psychological and psychosocial problems (see, for example, Gan & Schuller, 2002, le Roux, 2008).

Support groups

In larger cities in the US many aphasic couples find their way to speech therapy clinics, and more often than not, to group treatment and support groups. Groups have a number of functions for aphasics and their caregivers. It provides a community of peers with shared experiences, and it is a resource for services, research studies, treatment, and the like. Some groups are specifically designed as therapy groups and provide aphasics with a safe group setting where communication is encouraged and where aphasics have role models and peer support. Other groups are designed to provide emotional support to aphasics, caregivers or both.

Parr, Byng and Gilpin point out how important the setting is in communication when language is impaired – they talk about "the effect of context on meeting with others". (1997, p.119). Because of the language difficulties, aphasics have to rely on pre-established forms of contact which have been set up by others, and the context can affect the ethos of encounters with others. For example in the hospital ward shortly after the stroke or injury emphasis is on recovery from illness and treatment. In the rehabilitation setting, emphasis is on treatment and making progress. Support groups (and one can argue therapy groups) reduce isolation and brings a sense of being supported.

During a conference of the National Aphasia Association in Boston in 2006 various speakers who talked about aphasia therapy and support groups referred to the way in which these groups prepare people to participate in the "real world". Yet, as a participant remarked, for many of these people, the aphasia community is much more of a "real world", where they feel comfortable interacting, and less isolated, than the broader world the speakers were referring to. This participant questioned the assumption that the aphasia community, because it is has a specific focus, i.e. support and/or therapy of aphasics, is somehow unnatural or abnormal.

It seems that in terms of Goffman's conceptual scheme, support groups provide an alternative stage, which is different from that of the day-to-day environment in which aphasics create or manage impression. One could argue that, because these groups consist of peers and that the aphasics comprise a special kind of team. It provides already established fronts for new members to fit in. "When an actor takes on an established social role, usually he finds that a particular front has already been established for it" (Goffman, 1959, p.17) – in the case of aphasic/stroke survivor that front has not necessarily been established in "regular society" – by going to support groups and attending aphasia community group discovers the front that has been established by the group.

This is done in a number of ritualistic ways, demonstrating Goffman's point that fronts become institutionalized. For example, during every monthly meeting of a large Boston aphasia group my husband (who has aphasia) and I have attended since his accident in 2002, new members are asked to introduce themselves in front of the larger group. Typically these are people who have had recent strokes. The audience

meets their stories with nods, agreement, and comments of encourage-
ment. Someone inevitably advises them not to believe the common medical prognosis which states that recovery plateaus after six months. If they
have not already shared this information, they will be asked to tell about
their lives before and after the stroke (or head injury). When new members are met informally during the break it is very typical for old and new
members to share the stories about the onset of their strokes – the time,
place and date. Older members will reinforce the notion that "that was
then, and this is now" – there is a new reality and the implication is that
the sooner one adapts to the new stage, the more successful one will be at
managing it. This is an observation borne out by others (see, for example,
Hale, 2007, p.64).

Presentations by older members during these meetings provide
the model for behavior: for example, at one meeting, Dr.B. talks about a
road trip he took on his own. In his presentation of photographs, routes
travelled and experiences on the way, he is assisted by his wife. Although
he has difficulty communicating and navigating the PowerPoint used for
this presentation, and she is clearly the author of the presentation, everyone is very careful to direct their questions at him, and to applaud him for
his courage and presentation. Thus the front is presented to all members
and the idealization referred to above in the context of marriage (previous
section) is maintained. The key to impression management is to present
a sense of self to the audience that is strong enough for the audience to
define the actors as the actors want them to (Ritzer and Goodman, 2004,
p.224) – in the case of Dr. B, his wife assists him in his presentation of self,
and the audience are collaborating in the process by acting as if he were
the presenter.

Groups allow one to rehearse the front and perfect a routine without the cost of absolute failure. This allows one to feel confidence in larger
circles. The front is performed and practiced.

In the planning phase of the 2006 Speak Out Conference of the National Aphasia Association in Boston referred to above, members of the
different aphasia groups in the Boston area were invited to planning committees. In many cases I observed that their participation in these committees was nominal at most, but the impression was created that they were
involved in the planning of the conference. During the conference itself
speech therapists and spouses prepared aphasics to introduce the speakers. Again the audience collaborated in the process of impression management. As Goffman says, control of the setting is an advantage during
interaction – thus support groups become very important for aphasics
and their spouses, since it provides a controlled setting. The audience acts
in "respectful fashion, in awed regard for the sacred integrity imputed to
the performer" (Goffman, 1959, p.69).

Ironically, whereas the purpose of a support group is to allow a safe space (a true back region, in Goffman's language), this is not necessarily the case. During monthly meetings of a group in Boston, the breakout group with caregivers is strictly and exclusively limited to caregivers only, and this rule is aggressively enforced. No visitors, speech and language therapists, students or any other person is allowed to attend this meeting. In this way members feel safe to share their frustrations on the back stage. One participant in a group discussion described how worried she is every time her husband drives himself somewhere in the car, yet she never shares this concern with him. Another member tells many tales of going to restaurants or Irish pubs with her husband, and how confused the wait staff are because he does not appear disabled, yet insists on talking to them and ordering his own food and drink with great difficulty. Other members describe different strategies to make their spouses feel as if they are still the main decision-maker, or somehow "in charge" of their own lives, even though there is, within the safety of this support group, the admission that this is a pretence.

Yet even in this group discussion remains upbeat. One member, A., repeatedly tries to open discussion about "the things we never want to talk about", including sexual relationships, yet even when a discussant becomes tearful or expresses frustration, the tone of the group is upbeat. The silence that meets a male caregiver whose wife is in a nursing home rather than at home is palpable and, not surprisingly, he does not return to this group. The caregivers find it very difficult to divorce themselves from the societal expectation. In Goffman's terms the tension between what people expect us to do and what we may want to do spontaneously remains unresolved.

Conclusions

Goffman's work provides a useful framework for understanding the lives of aphasics and their caregiver-spouses. Aphasics have to create impression in new roles they have not rehearsed for, without the benefit of language. They are dependent on their spouse-caregivers to create impression together, as a team. Unfortunately the team does not provide a true back region for spouses. Support groups provide aphasics and their spouses with a script or front, which idealizes the relationship in terms of traditional gender roles and societal expectations of support and loyalty. Although support groups act, to some extent, as back region, it reinforces (institutionalizes) the idealized impressions. Support groups provide support and the sense of being part of a team for aphasics, yet spouses are primarily acting in the front region, maintaining or creating an impression of "normality". Ultimately aphasia impacts impression management of people with aphasia, requiring significant audience participation in this process, and it puts great demands on caregiver spouses/partners to be in the front region in public but also in the privacy of family and marital relationship.

References

Bullingham, L. & Vasconcelos, A.C. (2013). 'The presentation of self in the online world': Goffman and the study of online identities. *Journal of Information Science*. 39 (1), 101-112.

Crimmons, C. (2000). *Where is the Mango Princess? A Journey back from Brain Injury*. New York: Vintage Books.

Family Caregiver Alliance (2016). *Caregiver statistics: demographics*. https://www.caregiver.org/caregiver-statistics-demographics

Ganzfield, E.S. (2016). Let's talk about aphasia. In Greenfeld, M. & Ganzfield, E.S. (Eds.). *The word escapes me: voices of aphasia*. Bloomington: Balboa Press.

Goffman, E. (1959). *The Presentation of Self in Everyday Life*. New York: Anchor Books.

Goffman, E. (1963). *Stigma. Notes on the management of spoiled identity*. New York: Anchor Books.

Greenfeld, M. (2016). The new normal: recovery and healing. In Greenfeld, M. & Ganzfield, E.S. (Eds.). *The word escapes me: Voices of aphasia*. Bloomington: Balboa Press.

Hale, S. (2007). *The Man Who Lost His Language. A Case of Aphasia*. London: Jessica Kingsley Publisher.

Hogan, B. (2010). The presentation of self in the age of social media: Distinguishing performances and exhibitions online. *Technology and Society*. 30(6), 377-386.

Holland, A.L. (1998). Functional outcome assessment of aphasia following left hemisphere stroke. *Seminars in Speech and Language*. 19(3), 249-59.

Kirshner, H.S. (1995). Introduction to aphasia. In Kirshner, E. *Handbook of Neurological Speech and Language Disorders*. New York: Marcel Dekker.

le Roux, T. (2008). The private and the public: Family ideology and care of people with disabilities. *Women's Health and Urban Life. An Interna-*

tional and Interdisciplinary Journal. 7 (2), 16-30.

Maloney, C.M. (2013). *Finding my voice with aphasia. Walking through aphasia.* Bloomington: iUniverse.

Marks, L.M. (2017). *A stitch of time. The year a brain injury changed my language and life.* New York, NY: Simon & Schuster Paperbacks.

Menifee, C. L. (2000). *Aphasia. Research Summary.* http://www.selfcraft.net/HEALTH/Text.pdf

Mills, H. (2004). *A Mind of My Own. Memoir of recovery from Aphasia.* Bloomington: AuthorHouse.

Mitchell, N. (2018). *After Words.* Amazon Original Stories.

Montgomery-West, P. (1995). A spouse's perspective on life with aphasia. *Topics in Stroke Rehabilitation.* 2(3), 1-4.

National Aphasia Association. *Communication tips.* https://www.aphasia.org/aphasia-resources/communication-tips/

https://www.ninds.nih.gov/Disorders/All-Disorders/Aphasia-Information-Page

National Stroke Association (2018). http://www.strokeassociation.org/STROKEORG/AboutStroke/Impact-of-Stroke-Stroke-statistics_UCM_310728_Article.jsp#.W9HUefZRfIU

Paisley-Williams, K. (2017). *Where the Light Gets In: Losing My Mother Only to Find Her Again.* New York: Penguin Random House.

Parr, S., Byng, S., & Gilpin, S. (1997). *Talking about aphasia. Living with loss of language after stroke.* Buckingham: Open University Press.

Ritzer, G. and Goodman, D. J. (2004). *Modern sociological theory.* Boston: McGraw-Hill.

Schultz, C.C. (2010). *Crossing the void. My aphasia journey. Learning English the second time around.* Bellingham, WA: Chuckanut Enterprises.

Wulf, H. H. (1979). *Aphasia, my world alone.* Detroit: Wayne State University Press.

Zion, L. 2005. Finding another voice: moments of wonder. Newtonville, MA: Leonard Zion.

Chapter Four

Multiracial Families and the Intersectionality of Mental Health and Social Justice in the Foster Care System

Karmen R. Smith

Kevin P. Lyness

Antioch University New England

Existing marriage and family therapy (MFT) literature emphasizes a need for real-world preparation of intensive, community-based work collaboration, including in-home therapy and multidisciplinary services (Drury, Cocking, Beale, Hanson & Rapley, 2005; Gehart & Lucas, 2007; Ivey & Collins, 2003; Jager et al., 2009; Myers, Sweeney, & White, 2002; Nelson, Mitrani & Szapocznik, 2000). Additionally, facilitating healing within the family system requires an understanding of the intersectionality of complex family dynamics and the broader sociological contexts in which they are embedded. Parents of adoptive and foster children often turn from one expert to the next, in search of a solution to their child's dilemma. These foster and adoptive children often present with a variety of clinical issues, such as posttraumatic stress and behavioral problems, and have a 10-25% increased risk of placement disruption before the adoption has been legalized (Rampage et al., 2012). Preparation and additional collaborative efforts are needed to address the additional challenges that arise within the family as a function of the unique circumstance of adoption.

The term *special needs* was first introduced in the Child Abuse Prevention and Treatment and Adoption Reform Act of 1978 and was defined as characteristics of a child that could make adoption more difficult (Hansen, 2007). According to the federal government, the term special needs is used to describe adoptable children who are either (a) over the age of 5 years; (b) from a minority background; (c) physically, emotionally, or developmentally disabled; or (d) part of a sibling group, all of whom are eligible for adoption (Public Law 96-272, Federal Register, 1980). Though funding was small, the Adoption Reform Act of 1978 contained the first federal adoption incentive that funded state promotion in the adoption of children with special needs. In an effort to continue promoting the adoption of children with special needs from foster care, the federal government created the Adoption Assistance and Child Welfare Act of 1980 (Hansen, 2007). This Welfare Act of 1980 "amended section IV-E of the Social Security Act to authorize monthly adoption assistance payments to families adopting children who have special needs" (Hansen, 2007, p. 378). The Tax Relief Act of 2001 provided a $10,000 unqualified tax credit for families who adopt children with special needs (Hansen, 2007). This incentive from the federal government for prospective families serves as a tax benefit for families that are managing the extra care and sometimes hidden cost of adopting a child with special needs, including African American children.

As of July 2014, there were 402,378 children in the care system, 24% of whom identify as African American (U.S. Department of Health and Human Services, Administration for Children and Families, 2014). When viewing the care system as a measure of social policy and attitudes towards children, the number of children in care is reflective of the ineffectiveness of current policies and family support systems. Despite protransracial adoption laws, and increases in multiracial adoptive families across the United States, multiracial adoptive families continue to navigate a litany of public opinions and politics attached to their family system (Trenka, Oparah, & Shin, 2006). How do we, as mental health professionals, lead or assist in supporting a system transformation that accounts for the cultural adaptation of research, policy and practice when meeting the needs of adoptive African American children and families? The purpose of this paper is to explore how mental health professionals can address intersections of mental health and social justice while supporting a system transformation that accounts for the cultural adaptation of research, policy and practice when meeting the needs of adoptive African American children and families.

Collaboration across Systems

Best practices for foster care can emerge from the collaborative efforts of therapists, social services, and legal professionals within the court system (Britner & Mossler, 2002). This collaboration movement is requesting professionals across systems to trouble the impact of laws and policies on foster and adoptive families. McWey, Henderson and Tice (2006) called for helping professionals to join in a collaborative effort to develop best care practices when working with families involved in the foster care system and for MFTs, specifically, to increase their knowledge and understanding of current foster care policies and practices. Their purpose in conducting this qualitative investigation was to identify how the Adoption and Safe Families Act (ASFA) informed decision making, to recognize trends in decisions regarding the termination of parental rights of parents with mental health issues, and to explore treatment issues of families involved in the foster care system (McWey, Henderson & Tice, 2006). Implications from this grounded theory research study provide a framework based on awareness, assessment, and treatment when working with the adoptive population. By working together, therapists can increase their knowledge of current practices, gain experience on how to work effectively within the legal system, and witness how the term *special needs* shapes outcomes.

It is the responsibility of the community-based care or the adoption staff of the sub-contractor agency to inform prospective adoptive parents of the availability of all adoption benefits. According to a report from Voice for Adoption (2009), potential adoptive families and adoptive families report that there are not enough community supports to meet the needs of their families. Identified supports include support groups, crisis intervention, family counseling, and respite care (Voice for Adoption, 2009). Post-adoption services are temporary, yet these "services for families that adopt special needs children have been identified as key to achieving stability in these placements" (Carnochan, Moore & Austin, 2013, p. 214). While adoption-competent service providers are preferred to provide these services, MFTs are in prime positions to assist families in connecting with resources and other helping professionals while providing continued care.

In regards to the provision of mental health diagnoses, researchers are calling for the adjustment of current MFT practices (Gehart & Lucas, 2007; Kiselica & Robinson, 2001; Nelson et al., 2000). "Successful advocacy requires the ability to make differential diagnoses and justify these diagnoses with other professionals in the system" (Gehart & Lucas, 2007, p. 53). Knowledge and skills in diagnostic assessment related to mental health are essential for advocating in a complex social service system. Gehart and Lucas (2007) present the notion of advocacy in a refreshing way: advocacy as an attitude. By conducting their study from the client's perspective, these researchers further develop the definition of advocacy, stating it is "a commitment to consider the family and the broader system in which they and their problems are embedded and enacted" (Gehart & Lucas, 2007, p. 54).

When working with adoptive/foster population, it is important for therapists to develop a clear understanding of how professional opinions and the use of assessments influence outcomes for these families. For example, McWey, Henderson and Tice (2006) report that only two (6%) of the court cases in their study mentioned a therapist seeing the parent and child together before testifying about parental fitness when determining whether rights should be terminated. Benjet, Azar, and Kuersten-Hogan (2003) assert the importance of assessing parental behaviors in context when determining competence. However, there are further instances when therapists did not conduct parent-child assessments during their process of determining parental fitness and the termination of parental rights (McWey, Henderson, &Tice, 2006). It is both essential and ethically necessary for foster care agency workers to have as much information as possible when building a legal case to determine reunification or termination of parental rights. Insufficient knowledge along with insufficient competency in the medical model may hinder a therapist's attempts to place an attitude of advocacy in action.

Preparing Future Professionals

Current literature explores the question of how and to what degree professional associations similar to the Commission on Accreditation of Marriage and Family Therapy Education (COAMFTE) clinical training requirements prepare MFTs to navigate larger social contexts and collaborate across systems (Gehart & Lucas, 2007; Jager et al., 2009). There is a movement embedded in our current literature to expand the practice of counseling from its traditional focus on the intra-psychic concerns of clients to a broader focus on the many extra-psychic forces that adversely affect the emotional and physical well-being of people (Gehart & Lucas, 2007; Kiselica & Robinson, 2001). Lewis (2011) draws from structural and other post-modern therapies to offer guiding suggestions on how therapists can work with the families of this population. The suggested interventions, questions, and case examples further emphasize the importance of therapists enacting a truly systemic process by intervening in the larger system as fluidly as in the therapy room (Imber-Black, 1998; Lewis, 2011). While this movement is rapidly gaining momentum in the academic sphere, the process of filtration to the frontline professionals working with the adoptive and foster care population remains slow and fragmented.

Gehart (2012a) identified and described a shift in mental health treatment and outlines steps in the reformation of service provision to people diagnosed with severe mental illness. This paradigm shift views recovery as an alternative to the medical model for conceptualizing mental illness. This recovery model has an overarching ecological perspective and includes the following elements: (a) person-centered, (b) re-authoring, (c) exchange-centered, and (d) community-centered (Gehart, 2012a). She further identified the steps California has implemented to meaningfully transform their public mental health system and add training in recovery-oriented approaches to the MFT curriculum. This recovery model represents a significant paradigm shift, one that demonstrates methods of collaboration both with the consumer and across systems.

According to Voice for Adoption (2009), "adoptive families report that there is a continuing need for an established set of principles for adoption-competent mental health services" (p. 4). However, due to lack of funding and the scarcity of evidence-based research on post-adoption service models, there is little to assist with service evaluation and service model development (Voice for Adoption, 2009). Members of the Voice for Adoption (2009) coalition advocate for the following:

- The development and clear identification of best practice standards for working with adopted children and their families in post-adoption, mental health, or other service provision settings,
- The performance of outcome-based research that evaluates post-adoption service models and enhances best practice standards, and
- The collaboration of Child Welfare and Medicaid agencies to support the training of mental health practitioners on these standards.

Adoptive families report multiple struggles in finding and accessing adoption-competent community-based supports to meet their children's needs and stabilize their families (Voice for Adoption, 2009).

Adoptive families are outspoken about the unintentional harm caused by mental health providers when these professionals do not understand the dynamics and impact of adoption and previous trauma on children's overall development (Voice for Adoption, 2009). Strides made by multiple counseling professions to raise awareness of social justice issues include a call for ways in which therapists can use their position of power to advocate for change and assist the families of this population. MFTs could address this unintentional harm and establish themselves as a beneficial resource for these families by increasing their level of competence in working with this population. The following are some programs that offer a 64-hour curriculum, or 8 day training, on both foundational and clinical issues that arise when working with foster or adopted children and their families: Rutgers University in New Brunswick, New Jersey; Catawba County Department of Social Services, North Carolina; Lilliput Children's Services, Northern California, and the University of Minnesota reaching the Duluth/Twin Cities areas. The North American Council on Adoptable Children (NACAC) also offers trainings with the option to purchase the curriculum and receive additional instruction on how to provide future trainings for other supports within the community.

Clark, Thigpen and Yates (2006) conducted a qualitative, grounded theory study to identify the process of integrating adoptive children with special needs into the family, with implications for training future professionals. The theory that emerged consisted of a core category, *Developing a Sense of Family,* and two categories, *Decision to Adopt* and *Adjustment.* The Family Narrative Paradigm informed and was informed by the classifications identified in the study and provided a scheme through which the researchers integrated the process and structure of the categories (Clark et al., 2006). The emergent theory emphasized perception over actual behaviors and highlighted the importance of viewing behaviors in context. Suggested action steps resulting from this theory include: (a) assessing for and teaching good parenting skills; (b) utilizing techniques of reframing to view behaviors in context; (c) finding strengths, normalizing, and re-storying the family narrative; and (d) informing the placement of children with challenging behaviors (Clark et al., 2006, p. 191).

Advocacy and Social Justice

Researchers call for an "active commitment to issues of social justice, cultural competence, self of the therapist reflection, and collaboration [across disciplines] in MFT training programs" (Jager et al., 2009, p. 53) to better serve families involved in larger social systems. Jager et al. (2009) further discussed the ethical struggle of balancing advocacy and therapy, and privilege and oppression. Included in their study are incidents when some participatory therapists "moved into a position of advocacy, knowing that it had direct repercussions for the delivery of therapy services, relationships with caseworkers, collaboration, and the court process" (Jager et al., 2009, p. 52). These issues of difference and power where those in power view the powerless in a negative light can easily prevent successful outcomes (Pinderhughes, 1997). For example, Lewis (2011) describes how she was able to integrate her knowledge of systems theory and her experience within the care system to avoid a possible power struggle between the caseworkers and legal professionals involved in the case. According to Lewis (2011), "advocating for opportunities for Mr. Edwards to be more involved in making decisions for and spending more time with his son would be more helpful than...discounting the experiences of other professionals [and] inadvertently contribute to case stagnation..." (p. 440).

Gehart and Lucas (2007) further state, "when therapists advocate for clients in traditional and untraditional ways, clients learn to advocate effectively and appropriately for themselves" (p. 51). These methods of self-advocacy are represented in the social justice movements that promote consumer rights for persons diagnosed with a mental illness and are often the catalyst for the initiation of recovery-oriented models (Davidson et al., 2009). The incidents discussed in Jager et al. (2009) are further examples of how the intersectionality of mental health and issues of social justice influence the multi-stressed families engaged in the child welfare system.

A further goal of Jager and colleagues (2009) was to contribute additional information on methods to translate this increased education and awareness of advocacy and social justice into action. These authors derived the following implications for future practice: advocacy and empowerment, the system, the trenches, privilege and identity. In line with the interests of participatory action research (PAR), these interconnected themes assist in disambiguating the intersection of both micro- and macro-level social structures while also informing future practice. Their study and the resulting implications are just one example of how mental health professionals can use their position of privilege for change, thereby adopting an attitude of advocacy.

Conclusion

The wider questions of social justice and equality should be included in all discussions about families in the care system. African American children are categorized as special needs and are often accompanied by subsidy funding upon completion of the adoption process, yet they remain overly represented in the care system (Rampage et al, 2012; U.S. Department of Health and Human Services, Administration for Children and Families, 2014). Furthermore, our society has an increasing number of multiracial adoptive families that experience additional challenges, yet there are few adoption competent therapists who attend to issues of social injustice.

Families involved in foster care need culturally competent therapists who are willing to engage birth parents, foster parents, and the team of service providers in collaborative efforts to minimize postplacement trauma, and repair family connections while working towards permanent placement or reunification. As the number of MFTs involved in the care system increases, so too should the amount of communication and collaboration across professions. Possible evidence of an enacted collaborative care approach would demonstrate a direct correlation between the increase in the number of MFTs involved in the care system and the level of communication across professional fields. Too few helping professionals have devoted their time and talents to gain an understanding of the foster care system and the implications of the laws and policies on the families involved in that system. It is time for our professional community to advocate for the creation and implementation of initiatives that minimize siloing and promote a truly holistic model of treatment that addresses intersectionality by requiring cross-professional collaboration.

The Title IV-E subsidy provides access to resources post-adoption, and if MFTs are willing, there is an opportunity to increase one's competence and fulfill the desperate need identified by the families of this population. MFTs could conduct research on ways to help families overcome the unexpected challenges that arise post-adoption, after the discontinuation of a majority of the families' supports and financial resources. MFTs could also participate in research directed at highlighting how the lack of funding for post-adoption services places families at a disadvantage and creates additional cost to the care system due to failed placements.

Enacting a culturally competent practice means moving past an awareness of different cultures and racism and critically evaluating how personal beliefs, cultural differences and racism influences the decision making process when determining parental fitness. We, as a field of helping professionals, are in a prime position to bring awareness to the complex intersection between mental health, social justice, and the other respective needs of the populations we serve. Multiracial families, in particular, experience multi-systemic challenges that cannot be separated out from the larger socio-political systems. Nor can MFTs work with families of this population without addressing some of the most fundamental challenges of our society. Preparing MFTs to navigate larger social contexts and collaborate across systems while advocating for social justice are some of the ways to support a system transformation that accounts for the cultural adaptation of research, policy and practice when meeting the needs of adoptive African American children and families.

References

Benjet, C., Azar, S. T., & Kuersten-Hogan, R. (2003). Evaluating the parental fitness of psychiatrically diagnosed individuals: Advocating a functional-contextual analysis of parenting. *Journal of Family Psychology, 17,* 238 – 251.

Britner, P. A., & Mossler, D. G. (2002). Professional's decision-making about out-of-home placements following instances of child abuse. *Child Abuse and Neglect, 26,* 317 – 332.

Carnochan, S., Moore, M., & Austin, M. J. (2013). Achieving timely adoption. *Journal of Evidence-Based Social Work, 10,* 210-219. doi:10.1080/15433714.2013.788950

Clark, P., Thigpen, S., & Yates, A. M. (2006). Integrating the older/special needs adoptive child into the family. *Journal of Marital and Family Therapy, 32 (2),* 181 – 194.

Davidson, L., Tondora, J., O'Connell, M. J., Lawless, M. S., & Rowe, M. (2009). *A practical guide to recovery-oriented practice: Tools for transforming mental health care.* New York: Oxford University Press.

Drury, J., Cocking, C., Beale, J., Hanson, C., & Rapley, F. (2005). The phenomenology of empowerment in collective action. *British Journal of Social Psychology, 44,* 309-328. doi:10.1348/014466604X18523

Federal Register. (1980, June 17). Public Law No. 96-272: The adoption assistance and child welfare act of 1980. Retrieved March 4, 2015, from http://www.acf.hhs.gov/programs/cb/resource/pgm8101

Gehart, D. R. (2012a). The mental health recovery movement and family therapy, part I: Consumer-led reform of services to persons diagnosed with severe mental illness. *Journal of Marital and Family Therapy, 38 (3),* 429 – 442.

Gehart, D. R. (2012b). The mental health recovery movement and family therapy, part II: A collaborative appreciative approach for supporting mental health recovery. *Journal of Marital and Family Therapy, 38 (3),* 443 – 457.

Gehart, D. R., & Lucas, B. M. (2007). Client advocacy in marriage and family therapy: A qualitative case study. *Journal of Family Psychotherapy, 18* (1), 39-56. doi: 10.1300?J085v18n01_04

Hansen, M. E. (2007). Using subsidies to promote the adoption of children from foster care. *Journal of Family and Economic Issues, 28,* 377-393.

Hansen, M. E. & Pollack, D. (2005). Unintended consequences of bargaining for adoption assistance payments. *Family Court Review, 43* (3), p. 494–510.

Imber-Black., E. (1988). *Families and larger systems: A family therapist's guide through the labyrinth.* New York: Guilford Press.

Ivey, A. E., & Collins, N. M. (2003). Social justice: A long-tern challenge for counseling psychology. *The Counseling Psychologist, 31,* 290-300. doi: 10.1177/0011000003031003004

Jager, K. B., Bak, J., Barber, A., Bozek, K., Bocknek, E. L., & Weir, G. (2009). Qualitative inquiry and family therapist identity construction through community-based child welfare practice. *Journal of Feminist Family Therapy, 21,* 39-57. doi: 10.1080/08952830802683640

Kiselica, M. S. & Robinson, M. (2001). Bringing advocacy counseling to life: The history, issues, and human dramas of social justice work in counseling. *Journal of Counseling & Development, 79*, 387-397.

McWey, L.M., Henderson, T.L., & Tice, S. N. (2006). Mental health issues and the foster care system: An examination of the impact of the adoption and safe families act. *Journal of Marital and Family Therapy, 32 (2)*, 195 – 214.

Myers, J. E., Sweeney, T. J., & White, V. E. (2002). Advocacy for counseling and counselors: A professional imperative. *Journal of Counseling and Development, 80*, 394-402.

Nelson, R. H., Mitrani, V. B., & Szapocznik, J. (2000). Applying a family-ecosystemic model to reunite family separated due to child abuse: A case study. *Contemporary Family Therapy*, 125-149.

Pinderhughes, E. B. (1997). The interaction of difference and power as a basic framework for understanding work with African Americans: Family theory, empowerment and educational approaches. *Smith College Studies in Social Work, 67(3)*, 323–347.

Rampage, C., Eovaldi, M., Ma, C., Foy, C. W., Samuels, G. M., & Bloom, L. (2012). Adoptive families. In F. Walsh (Ed.), *Normal family processes: Growing diversity and complexity* (4th ed., pp. 222-246). New York, NY: Guilford Press.

Sedlak, A. J, & D.D. Broadhurst (1993). *Study of adoption assistance impact and outcomes: Final report.* Rockville, MD: Westat, Inc.

Trenka, J. J., Oparah, J. C., & Shin, S. Y. (2006). *Outsiders within: Writing on transracial adoption.* Cambridge, MA: South End Press.

U.S. Department of Health and Human Services, Administration for Children and Families. (2014). *The AFCARS Report* (21). Retrieved from Children's Bureau website: http://www.acf.hhs.gov/sites/default/files/cb/afcarsreport21.pdf

Voice for Adoption. (2009). *Encouraging adoption and helping families: The case for refocusing federal funding on postadoption services.* Retrieved from Voice for Adoption, Inc. website: https://www.google.com/url?sa=t&rct=j&q=&esrc=s&source=web&cd=1&ved=0ahUKEwi-0grrIlbnJAhVKKyYKHYY0DsAQFggdMAA&url=http%3A%2F%2Fvoice-for-adoption.org%2Fsites%2Fdefault%2Ffiles%2FV-FA%2520post-adopt%2520paper%2520FINAL%25207.9.09.pdf&usg=AFQjCNG77gGigf9PvJJeIjsK-xy_pJVwgw&cad=rja

Chapter Five

Inmates with Mental Illness in New York State Jails:

An Assessment

Daniela Peterka-Benton

Montclair State University

Patrick Johnson
Brian Paul Masciadrelli

The State University of New York at Fredonia

Mental Health Care Past and Present

The largest psychiatric institutions in the United States are no longer hospitals. When the deinstitutionalization movement closed state hospitals but failed to adequately meet the need for alternate community living and treatment options, correctional facilities became the replacement custodial care setting (Torrey, 2008). The United States faced a similar situation prior to the 1840s, with a majority of poor, mentally ill persons confined to poor houses at best, and to jails or prisons at worst (Grob, 1966, 1973). We have come full circle today, with the seriously mentally ill again being confined to jails and prisons much as they were 175 years ago (Peterka-Benton & Masciadrelli, 2013; Torrey, Kennard, Eslinger, Lamb, & Pavle, 2010).

Mental illness did not pose a significant social problem until the nineteenth century. The overall population of the colonies prior to that time was relatively small, and so the proportion of the population with mental illness was similarly small (Grob, 1966). The mid-1800s saw major changes in care for the mentally ill. Moral management became the vanguard of treatment, using structured activity and living environments to promote recovery from mental illness, and the state hospital would replace the penal institution as the setting where the mentally ill received care. Further fueling this was a belief that mental illness was curable (Fellin, 1996, Grob, 1966, Whitaker, 2002), creating a period of hope in the struggle with mental illness.

It became evident that mental illnesses were generally chronic, incurable disorders during the 1890s. State hospitals became orientated toward custodial care, leading to overpopulation by very long term residents. Correspondingly, the conditions within them gradually became increasingly impersonal and ultimately inhumane (Fellin, 1996). By mid-twentieth century state hospital care for the mentally ill was largely seen as a failure (Grob, 1973). As a result, the 1960s saw pivotal legislation, such as President Kennedy's Community Mental Health Centers Act of 1963, which facilitated the process known as deinstitutionalization (Torrey, 2013). Ultimately, long-term commitment to state hospitals would no longer be an option for managing mental illness. The seriously mentally ill would move out of state hospitals by the thousands, while inadequate community-based services, lack of options for long-term inpatient care, and public responses to mental illness directed at the criminal aspects of disturbed behavior would lead to large numbers of seriously mentally ill persons being incarcerated rather than hospitalized due to their illnesses (Torrey, 2008, 2013).

Today, the United States incarcerates the mentally ill in quantity. The situation bears undeniable likeness to the plight of the mentally ill in the 1840s, as the primary public health option for managing seriously mental illness is again a penal facility (Peterka-Benton & Masciadrelli, 2013; Torrey et al., 2010).

The Challenges of Housing Mentally Ill Inmates in Correctional Facilities

As various jails and prisons are faced with growing numbers of mentally ill inmates, the many problems of putting this particular population into correctional facilities becomes apparent. Problems frequently faced by these institutions include an increase in behavioral problems caused, vulnerability of mentally ill inmates to abuses, increased suicide risk, and more time spend in solitary confinement (Treatment Advocacy Center, 2014). While all correctional facilities face the same or similar problems housing mentally ill inmates, Olley, Nicholls and Brink (2009) point out that county jails carry a greater burden since they not only house convicted offenders, but also mentally ill individuals awaiting transfer to a mental health facility among other pre-trial detainees. Looking at convicted inmates, many mentally ill offenders are charged with minor misdemeanor crimes caused by criminal behavior often tied to the mental illness (Etter, Birzer & Fields, 2008). Compared to state or federal correctional facilities, county jails do not receive a steady stream of funds to address the specific needs of the mentally ill population. Instead they have to rely on the local tax revenue, which may or may not be able to pay for treatment and increased security needs (Dalley, 2014). Regardless of the type of correctional facility, it is critical to acknowledge that the criminal justice system was never designed to become the primary service provider for the mentally ill (Gondles, 2005), and therefore many problems of housing this particular inmate population are common to all correctional facilities.

A primary concern for all correctional facilities that house mentally ill inmate populations is the provision of adequate treatment services for rehabilitation. This concerns not only the primary diagnoses of mental illness, but also the treatment of co-occurring disorders and correlating traumas (Dalley, 2014). Studies have found that substantial numbers of county jail inmates with mental health issues also display substance abuse problems (Young, 2003; Ditton, 1999; Teplin, Abram, & McClelland, 1996). Given the limited resources correctional facilities receive to address the needs of their mentally ill inmates, Adams and Ferrandino (2008) note that medications are administered as the only form of treatment, sometimes to treat the underlying illness, but often to keep those inmates calm to make work easier for correctional staff.

The stressful environment of overcrowded jails and prisons creates increased risks for self-inflicted injuries and suicide among mentally ill inmates. Suicide is common among inmates with mental health problems when untreated. According to Dalley (2014), suicide was the second leading cause of jail inmate deaths in 2011, which represents a very serious challenge as more and more mentally ill individuals enter the correctional system. Deteriorating conditions in many correctional facilities also lead to greater victimization of mentally inmates. Mentally ill inmates are significantly more likely to be physically and sexually victimized than other inmates as they are more vulnerable because of dependence on others, lack social skills to interact adequately with the general prison or jail population, and greater needs for attention than do healthy inmates (Vogel, Stephens, & Siebels, 2014). Mentally ill individuals also tend to have a hard time following the many rules and regulations that dictate prison life and are often faced with disciplinary action at a higher rate than the rest of the population. Aside from rule violations, mentally ill inmates can also become violent against other prisoners or staff, which may place them in secure units isolated from other inmates in a high-control environment (O'Keefe, 2007; James & Glaze, 2006).

Administrative segregation, including maximum security facilities and isolation units, is used to control dangerous inmates and is characterized by long-term solitary confinement of the offender. Inmates with mental health issues are disproportionately represented in such high-control environments due to their behavioral issues in the general population, which are often a manifestation of their illness (Vogel et al., 2014; Arrigo and Bullock, 2008; O'Keefe & Schnell, 2007). Segregation can have harmful effects on any inmate, oftentimes manifesting in what became known as Special Housing Unit Syndrome (SHU-Syndrome), a term coined by psychiatrist Stuart Grassian (2006) in the early 1980s. Inmates not afflicted by a mental illness as they enter solitary confinement, might develop a variety of medical and psychological aliments including "severe and chronic depression, anxiety, problems with impulse control, self-mutilation, decreased brain function, hallucinations, and revenge fantasies" (Steinbuch, 2014, p. 501). The psychological effects on mentally ill inmates in solitary confinement, however, are even greater due to stress, lack of social interaction, and an unstructured daily routine (Johnston, 2013). Furthermore, inmates in solitary confinement are usually restricted from participation in treatment groups or any other kind of therapeutic programs, often exacerbating their symptoms, in turn only keeping them longer in administrative segregation, turning this process into a cycle impossible to escape. Looking at the disturbing effects solitary confinement can have, particularly on mentally ill inmates, discussions have surfaced suggesting that solitary confinement of this particular inmate group violates disability rights statutes (Glidden and Rovner, 2012), or even inmates' eighth amendment rights (Hafemeister and George, 2012).

The challenges continue for mentally ill individuals as they reach the end of their incarceration. According to Hannah-Moffat (2014), mentally ill inmates are less likely to be released on parole due to a greater number of infractions, often caused by their mental illness. An even greater obstacle results from inadequate aftercare planning as released inmates are to return back into the community. Without support in the community, mentally ill individuals may stop taking their medications, leading to a relapse in symptoms, which ultimately brings them back into the system. Several studies have shown that individuals with mental health problems are more likely to serve multiple prison or jail terms as compared to other inmates, and they also face sentences up to 15 months longer than inmates charged with similar offenses (Baillargeon, Binswanger, Penn, Williams & Murray, 2009, James & Glaze, 2006, Ditton, 1999). Ditton (1999) also found that lack of employment or social assistance for released offenders with a mental health problem represents serious obstacles and a major determinant of homelessness. Accompanying homelessness, problems such as substance abuse, limited access to medication, and criminal offending occur, setting many on a path back into the criminal justice system.

In conclusion, it can be determined that confining the mentally ill in prisons and jails not only creates many obstacles and challenges for the correctional system itself, but for those inmates and their specific mental health care needs as well.

Surveying County Jails of New York

While many correctional facilities serve as the nation's primary mental health care providers, summative and exhaustive data on the number of mentally inmates in the various facilities, their treatment options, and funding streams addressing the needs of mentally ill inmates are often not available. This is also the case for county jail facilities in New York, which are the focus of this study. Jails also provide an interesting field of study since they face the correctional mental health crisis more acutely with the heterogeneous mix of individuals that make up jail populations on any given day. People in a mental health crisis, who in the past could be taken in through the mental health system, now end up in the criminal justice system, with its first stop being the county jail. Jails are also an interesting sub-segment within the correctional sector to look at in terms of available funding to meet the needs of this growing inmate sector. No comprehensive data are available on inmates with diagnosed mental health problems, their treatment, or funding of programs to support the needs of this group in New York.

In order to gather information for a statewide assessment of county jail facilities, the project team constructed a semi-structured survey utilizing Survey Monkey to solicit descriptive information about the current status of mentally ill inmates in county jails throughout New York. It should be noted that this study was initiated prior to the introduction of DSM-5, therefore the survey used the multi-axial diagnostic system from DSM-IV-TR. The 8-question survey was first sent to Thomas Mitchell, Counsel of the New York State Sheriffs' Association, Inc., for distribution of the survey link to all 62 counties via Sheriffs' or jail administrators' email. Surveys were initially collected between January 6, 2014 and January 24, 2014, but the data collection period was extended by one week until January 31, 2014 to increase the response rate. Twenty-seven county jail administrators had provided full or partial information for the survey at the end of data collection, which resulted in a response rate of 43.5%.

A wide variety of psychiatric disorders have been observed among the incarcerated generally, with substance use disorders usually included among them. Two categories of psychiatric disorders tend to predominate in incarcerated populations once substance use disorders are discounted (James & Glaze, 2006), mood disorders and thought disorders. Further breakdown specifies major depressive disorder and manic episodes of bipolar disorder as the mood disorders, and disorders characterized frank psychotic symptoms, as found in schizophrenia, as the thought disorders.

There is variability in prevalence of these disorders depending on whether the facility is a federal prison, state prison, or county jail, with the greatest numbers found among county jails (James & Glaze, 2006). Major depressive disorder was found in 29.7 percent of inmates in county jails, while 23.5 percent of state prison inmates and only 16 percent of federal prison inmates presented with it. Likewise, manic episodes of bipolar disorder were reported in 54.5 percent of county jail inmates, and then in 43.2 percent of state prison inmates and 53.1 percent of federal prison inmates. Finally, psychotic disorders are again found most in county jails with these indicated in 23.9 percent of the inmates, but only 15.4 percent of state prison inmates and 10.2 percent of federal prison inmates (James & Glaze, 2006).

Prevalence findings like these point to the importance of inquiry into the disorders among county jail populations. Such high frequencies for county jails in comparison to other types of correctional facilities, especially with psychotic disorders, suggest that these facilities are a target for action in remedying problems with high rates of incarceration of the mentally ill. The survey was designed to collect descriptive information regarding the location of the respective jail facility and its current overall jail population. Respondents were asked to list the number of jail inmates who were diagnosed by mental health professionals with one of the following disorders as their primary diagnosis: Schizophrenia, Schizoaffective Disorder, Bipolar Disorder, Major Depressive Disorder, PTSD, other psychotic disorder, other mood disorder.

Other survey questions tried to identify how many of the inmates were diagnosed with more than one of any axis I disorders, as well as to identify the number of inmates who are diagnosed with a personality disorder (e.g., Antisocial, Borderline). Lastly, several questions try to shed some light on the actual treatment of these diagnosed inmates and funding streams for these types of mental health services.

Results

Out of 62 counties in New York that were contacted, 27 county jails responded to the survey, with 26 listing their actual name. Analysis of inmates with axis I disorders as their primary diagnoses reveals that Bipolar Disorder appears to be the most frequently diagnosed with 403 cases (5.0% of total jail population of all reporting facilities), followed by 278 cases of Major Depressive Disorder (3.5%), 275 cases of Schizophrenia (3.5%), 142 cases of other psychotic disorder (1.8%), 192 cases of PTSD (2.4%), and 134 cases of Schizoaffective Disorder (1.7%). There were 488 cases (6.0%) diagnosed with "another mood disorder", which was not further specified.

The number of inmates diagnosed with one axis I disorder varies from facility to facility, ranging from 5.6% to 79.4% of the total population at the respective facilities. This large variation in diagnosed individuals is somewhat surprising and raises the question whether the discrepancy truly is a result of varying numbers of mentally ill individuals, or if some inmates simply remain undiagnosed for reasons unknown.

Monroe County Jail	1308
Westchester County Dept. of Correction	1211
Albany County Correctional Facility	809
Onondaga County Justice Center	628
Oneida County Jail	500
Niagara County Correctional Facility	496
Ulster County Jail	348
Broome County Sheriffs Correctional Facility	452
Chautauqua County Jail	251
Ontario County Jail	224
Rockland County Correctional Facility	203
Cayuga County Jail	195
Steuben County Jail	183
Jefferson County Jail	174
Wayne County- New York	142
Livingston County Jail, Geneseo, NY	137
Allegany County Sheriff's Office	127
Franklin County Jail	127
Columbia County Jail	121
Putnam County Correctional Facility	114
Washington County Jail	114
Fulton County Jail	113
Madison County Jail	104
Seneca County	79
Wyoming County Jail	72
Yates County Jail	49

Table 1: Inmate population of surveyed facilities

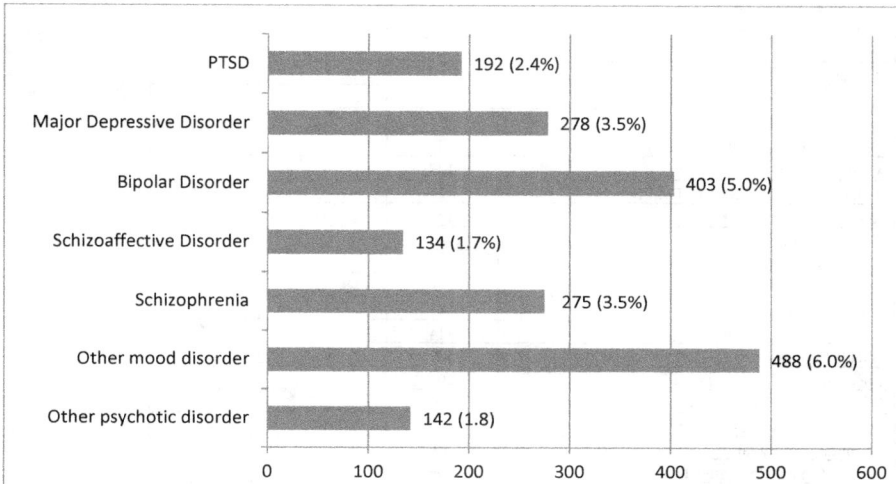

Table 2. Axis 1 disorders as primary diagnosis (n=8081)

In addition to axis I disorders, inmates are also frequently diagnosed with antisocial, borderline, or other personality disorders. While not all facilities diagnose these types of disorders, most respondents were able to provide some information on personality disorders among their inmates. Surveyed facilities reported up to 25.1% of their inmates to be diagnosed with antisocial personality disorder (4.7% across all reporting jails), up to 25.1% to be diagnosed with borderline personality disorder (2.6% across all reporting jails) and up to 40% to be diagnosed with other personality disorders (2.4% across all reporting jails). The fact that numerous inmates in New York county jails are diagnosed with axis I and/or personality disorders raises the question about how facilities address this particular inmate population in regards to treatment.

A significant obstacle correctional facilities face housing mentally ill inmates is the need to provide adequate treatment for them. All the surveyed facilities reported offering medication or counseling to inmates with diagnosed mental health problems. The vast majority of jails offered both. It should be noted that jail administrators, who reported no treatment for

	Jail Population	Total number of inmates with Axis 1 primary diagnosis	Percent of total jail population
Ontario County Jail	224	151	67.4
Columbia County Jail	121	72	59.5
Wayne County- New York	142	72	50.7
Franklin County Jail	127	59	46.5
Allegany Co. Sheriff's Office	127	57	44.9
Broome County Sheriffs Correctional Facility	452	200	44.2
Chautauqua County Jail	251	107	42.6
Livingston County Jail, Geneseo, NY *	137	57	41.6
Madison County Jail	104	42	40.4
Putnam County Correctional Facility	114	45	39.5
Jefferson County Jail	174	54	31.0
Yates County Jail	49	15	30.6
Ulster County Jail	348	98	28.2
Seneca County Jail	79	22	27.8
Fulton County Jail	113	31	27.4
Washington County Jail	114	31	27.2
Oneida County Jail	500	121	24.2
Rockland County Correctional Facility	203	44	21.7
Westchester County Dept. of Correction	1211	255	21.1
Onondaga County Justice Center	628	125	19.9
Wyoming County Jail	72	13	18.1
Niagara County Correctional Facility	496	86	17.3
Albany County Correctional Facility	809	61	7.5
Monroe County Jail	1308	83	6.3
Cayuga County Jail	195	11	5.6

* Not all inmates see Mental Health provider. MH sees only those who are referred, request it, or who have lethality crises.

Table 3. Inmates with Axis 1 disorders as primary diagnosis by facility

	Jail pop.	Antisocial personality disorder	Antisocial personality disorder (%)	Borderline personality disorder	Borderline personality disorder (%)	Other personality disorders	Other personality disorders (%)
Monroe County Jail	1308	12	0.9	5	0.4	1	0.1
Westchester Co. Dept. of Correction	1211	125	10.3	50	4.1	20	1.7
Albany Co. Correctional Facility	809	3	0.4	2	0.2	2	0.2
Onondaga Co. Justice Center	628	0	0.0	3	0.5	3	0.5
Oneida County Jail	500	55	11.0	48	9.6	0	0.0
Niagara Co. Correctional Facility	496	N/A	N/A	N/A	N/A	N/A	N/A
Ulster County Jail	348	12	3.4	2	0.6	3	0.9
Broome Co. Sheriffs Corr. Facility	452	N/A	N/A	N/A	N/A	N/A	N/A
Chautauqua County Jail	251	0	0.0	0	0.0	22	8.8
Ontario County Jail	224	5	2.2	2	0.9	16	7.1
Rockland Co. Correctional Facility	203	N/A	N/A	1	0.5	0	0.0
Cayuga County Jail	195	49	25.1	49	25.1	78	40.0
Steuben County Jail	183	N/A	N/A	N/A	N/A	N/A	N/A
Jefferson County Jail	174	25	14.4	5	2.9	3	1.7
Wayne County Jail	142	25	17.6	6	4.2	3	2.1
Livingston County Jail*	137	10	7.3	5	3.6	2	1.5
Allegany Co. Sheriff's Office	127	0	0.0	3	2.4	0	0.0
Franklin County Jail	127	13	10.2	4	3.1	4	3.1
Columbia County Jail	121	5	4.1	4	3.3	2	1.7
Putnam Co. Correctional Facility	114	4	3.5	6	5.3	6	5.3
Washington County Jail	114	N/A	N/A	N/A	N/A	N/A	N/A
Fulton County Jail	113	20	17.7	0	0.0	6	5.3
Madison County Jail	104	4	3.8	4	3.8	16	15.4
Seneca County Jail	79	11	13.9	6	7.6	0	0.0
Wyoming County Jail	72	0	0.0	0	0.0	0	0.0
Yates County Jail	49	5	10.2	3	6.1	6	12.2

* Not all inmates see Mental Health provider. MH sees only those who are referred, request it, or who have lethality crises.

Table 4. Number of inmates diagnosed with personality disorder by facility

certain disorders, usually listed extremely low numbers of individuals diagnosed with these disorders.

	No treatment	Medication only	Counseling/ therapy only	Medication and Counseling/Therapy	Total number of responding facilities
Schizophrenia	0 (0%)	5 (20%)	0 (0%)	20 (80%)	25
Schizoaffective Disorder	0 (0%)	4 (15.4%)	1 (3.8%)	21 (80.8%)	26
Bipolar Disorder	0 (0%)	4 (15.4%)	0 (0%)	22 (84.6%)	26
Major Depressive Disorder	0 (0%)	4 (15.4%)	0 (0%)	22 (84.6%)	26
PTSD	0 (0%)	3 (11.6%)	1 (3.8%)	22 (84.6%)	26
Other psychotic disorder	0 (0%)	4 (16.7%)	0 (0%)	22 (83.8%)	24
Other mood disorder	1 (3.8%)	4 (15.4%)	2 (7.7%)	19 (73.1%)	26
Antisocial personality disorder	2 (7.7%)	4 (15.4%)	1 (3.8%)	19 (73.1%)	26
Borderline personality disorder	2 (8.0%)	4 (16.0%)	2 (8.0%)	17 (68 %)	25
Other personality disorders	2 (8.0%)	4 (16.0%)	2 (8.0%)	17 (68 %)	25

Table 5. Treatments offered for specific diagnosed disorders by reporting facilities

As correctional facilities are turning into the country's largest mental health facilities, questions arise as to how to fund this continuously growing expense. While county mental health departments may appear to be the best source for such funding, the survey revealed that 50% of facilities that participated fund their mental health needs entirely through their own (Sheriff's) budget, while only 34.6% of them utilize county mental health funding to address the needs of their mentally ill jail population. This data shows how correctional facilities are faced with taking on that additional financial burden by turning them into the primary holding centers for mentally ill individuals in our society without providing adequate or additional funding streams to provide the much-needed mental health resources and treatments.

Source of funding	Correctional facilities using this type of funding
County Mental Health Department	9 (34.6%)
County Budget	3 (11.5%)
County and Sheriff's Budget combined	1 (3.9%)
Sheriff's Budget	13 (50.0%)

Table 6. Source of mental health funding (n=26)

Discussion

Academic research has looked at many problems correctional facilities face as the nation's largest mental health providers. Again and again we seem to draw the conclusion that correctional facilities are not an appropriate place to treat mentally ill individuals, yet immediate solutions to this problem seem to be nowhere near. County jails carry the heaviest burden as the first stop for every mentally ill person in conflict with the law, whether that be for evaluation, pre-trial detainment, or post-trial sentence. This study intended to provide a baseline assessment of mentally ill inmates inside New York's county jails by measuring the number of individuals diagnosed with major axis I and personality disorders.

One of the most concerning findings was that some facilities reported almost 80% of their entire population being diagnosed with at least one axis I disorder. While these might be outliers, all responding facilities reported one in three inmates on average to be diagnosed in this way.

Looking at the specific diagnoses, results reveal an interesting finding regarding bipolar disorder being the most frequently diagnosed axis I disorder, with major depressive disorder and schizophrenia being distant seconds. Based on these findings it appears that the services to control bipolar disorder in affected individuals should be more focused. While the current study does not delineate the nuances of this phenomenon, future research will focus on disentangling bipolar disorder from others in this population to better understand this problem.

The findings also reveal that all facilities provide some sort of treatment for their diagnosed inmates, with the majority of them providing care including medication or counseling, frequently both. This does not indicate a comprehensive program of services or continuum of care, which might be influenced by financial constraints.

The financial burden carried by correctional facilities housing mentally ill inmates can be tremendous, as supported by the results indicating that 50% of the reporting facilities do in fact rely solely on the Sheriff's own budget to care for those individuals. With half of the county jails reporting no financial assistance from their local mental health departments, it questions as to whether these mentally ill offenders are prepared for their eventual reentry back to their communities. If the facilities are merely stabilizing the inmates until their release, they are not taking the steps to ensure a continuum of care after the inmates leave the facility.

Due to these funding issues, jails face numerous related structural challenges when dealing with this inmate population, which might lead to possible cuts in correctional security operations, staff training, and programming for inmates. One major concern for all jails is the proper housing of the mentally ill, who may or may not be housed with the general population depending on their diagnoses. Larger facilities may have infirmaries available to provide the mentally ill with a less stressful environment, but smaller jails usually do not have the physical plant to separate inmates with special needs. All too often the only solution for inmates who are behaviorally acting out is to place them in solitary confinement, which is detrimental. At the same time, some mentally ill individuals may pose a threat to other inmates and staff, and therefore may need to be housed separately. Jail administrators are faced with such challenging decisions regularly, even though the role of a quasi-mental health director is not a traditional duty they are charged to perform.

Correctional officers today are faced with many more responsibilities than their predecessors, who were often turn keys or jail guards. Officers are responsible for correcting something, which we know is the behavior of those incarcerated in our jails. Unfortunately, the standards for formal education of correction officers have not kept up with the requirements of their positions. Officers who have obtained formal education in theories of corrections, sociology, and psychology can better serve the treatment side of the operations so that they can enhance the custody functions of their facilities. It is quite obvious that specialized mental health training is essential toward addressing inmate needs. Recognizing the important role correctional officers have in the rehabilitation of inmates is key, especially for those inmates with special needs. This alone requires specialized training that is much more in depth than the few hours dedicated in the current basic correction officer training course.

With recidivism rates still high, re-entry programs for inmates have become a much needed priority for all correctional facilities in order to allow released inmates to re-integrate into society. Proper reentry initiatives for inmates with mental health problems require a multidisciplinary team to begin treatment inside the facility and have an action plan in place for the offender prior to release. The local mental health departments need to lead this process and be more proactive in the treatment and funding of these programs inside the facility. Treatment programs inside the facilities should replicate the programs in the community in order for the inmates to receive the proper care. Further, a continuum of care coordinated between the jail and community mental health providers is essential for the offender being released so that he or she does not miss treatments, stop taking medication, slip back into disturbed states, commit crimes, and be re-incarcerated. Reentry programs for the mentally ill require an extensive action plan for the offender to follow and for providers to check the progress of their clients upon their return to the community. If we continue to neglect those very basic processes needed for re-entry success, we will have to accept the revolving door for mentally ill offenders.

It should be noted that this study only serves as a starting point for the discussion of mentally ill inmates in New York county jails due to the limited scope of the survey. It is understood that an in-depth analysis would require much more specific information on this topic. In this first attempt to develop baseline numbers on this inmate population, the research team decided not to overtax correctional institutions with a lengthy survey, but instead opt for a more limited scope in exchange for an expected higher response rate. While this is a limitation for the present study, it can serve as the basis for a series of follow-up studies to understand these trends over time.

References

Adams, K., & Ferrandino, J. (2008). Managing mentally ill inmates in prisons. *Criminal Justice and Behavior, 35*, 913–927.

Arrigo, B. A., & Bullock, J. L. (2008). The psychological effects of solitary confinement on prisoners in supermax units: Reviewing what we know and recommending what should change. *International Journal of Offender Therapy and Comparative Criminology, 52*, 622–40.

Baillargeon J., Binswanger I., Penn J., Williams B., & Murray O. (2009). Psychiatric disordrs and repeat incarcerations: The revolving prison door. *American Journal of Psychiatry, 166*, 103–9.

Dalley, L. P. (2014). From asylums to jails: The prevailing impact on female offenders. *Women & Criminal Justice, 24*, 209-228.

Ditton, P.M. (1999). *Mental health and treatment of inmates and probationers* (U.S. Department of Justice Publication No. NCJ 174463). Washington, DC: U.S. Government Printing Office.

Etter, G. W., Birzer, M. L., & Fields, J. (2008). The jail as a dumping ground: the incidental incarceration of mentally ill individuals. *Criminal Justice Studies, 21*, 79-89.

Fellin, P. (1996). *Mental health and mental illness: Policies, programs, and services.* Belmont, CA: Brooks/Cole.

Glidden, B. & Rovner, L. (2012). Requiring the state to justify supermax confinement for mentally ill prisoners: A disability discrimination approach. *Denver University Law Review, 90*, 55-75.

Gondles Jr., J. A. (2005, February). The mentally ill don't belong in jail. *Corrections Today*, p. 6.

Grassian, S. (2006). Psychiatric effects of solitary confinement. *Journal of Law & Policy, 22*, 325-383.

Grob, G. N. (1966). *The state and the mentally ill.* Chapel Hill: University of North Carolina.

Grob, G. N. (1973). *Mental institutions in America: Social policy to 1875.* New York: Free Press.

Hafemeister, T. L. & George, J. (2012). The ninth circle of hell: An eighth amendment analysis of imposing prolonged supermax solitary confinement on inmates with a mental illness. *Denver University Law Review, 1*, Virginia Public Law and Legal Theory Research Paper No. 2012-39.

Hannah-Moffat, K. (2004). Losing ground: Gendered knowledges, parole risk, and responsibility. *Social Politics: International Studies in Gender, State & Society, 11*, 363-385.

James, D. J., & Glaze, L. E. (2006). Mental health problems of prison and jail inmates (NCJ No. 213600). Washington, DC: Office of Justice Programs, Bureau of Justice Statistics, U.S. Department of Justice. Retrieved from http://bjs.ojp.usdoj.gov/ index.cfm?ty=pbdetail&iid=789.

Johnston, E. L. (2013). Vulnerability and just desserts: A theory of sentencing and mental illness. *Journal of Criminal Law & Criminology, 103,* 147-229.

O'Keefe, M. L. (2007). Administrative segregation for mentally ill inmates. *Journal of Offender Rehabilitation, 45,* 149–165.

O'Keefe, M. L., & Schnell, M. J. (2007). Offenders with Mental Illness in the Correctional System. *Journal of Offender Rehabilitation, 45,* 81-104.

Olley, M. J., Nicholls T. L., Brink J. (2009). Mentally ill individuals in limbo: Obstacles and opportunities for providing psychiatric services to corrections inmates with mental illness. *Behavioral Sciences & the Law, 27,* 811-831.

Peterka-Benton, D. & Masciadrelli, B. P. (2013). Legitimacy of corrections as a mental health care provider: Perspectives from U.S. and European systems. *The Journal of the Institute for Justice and International Studies, 13,* 171-184.

Steinbuch, A. T. (2014). The movement away from solitary confinement in the United States. *New England Journal on Criminal & Civil Confinement, 40,* 499-533.

Teplin, L. A., Abram, K. M., & McClelland, G. M. (1996). Prevalence of psychiatric disorders among incarcerated women. I. Pretrial jail detainees. *Archives of General Psychiatry, 53,* 505-512.

Torrey, E. F. (2008). *The insanity offense.* New York: Norton.

Torrey, E. F. (2013). *American psychosis.* New York: Oxford.

Torrey, E. F., Kennard, A. D., Eslinger, D., Lamb, R. & Pavle, J. (2010). *More Mentally Ill persons are in jail and Prison than Hospitals: A Survey of the States.* Treatment Advocacy Center. Retrieved from http://www.treatmentadvocacycenter.org/storage/documents/final_jails_v_hospitals_study.pdf

Treatment Advocacy Center (2014). The treatment of persons with mental illness in prisons and jails: a state survey. Retrieved from: http://www.tacreports.org/storage/documents/treatment-behind-bars/treatment-behind-bars.pdf

Vogel, M., Stephens, K. D., & Siebels, D. (2014). Mental illness and the criminal justice system. *Sociology Compass, 8,* 627-638.

Whitaker, R. (2002). *Mad in America.* Cambridge, MA: Perseus.

Young, D. (2003). Co-occurring disorders among jail inmates: Bridging the treatment gap. *Journal of Social Work Practice in the Addictions, 3,* 63-85.